RELATIONSHIP Rx

PRAISE FOR *RELATIONSHIP Rx*

"This book, authored by two outstanding experts, offers hope and practical help for couples dealing with troubled relationships and trying to find authentic and meaningful intimacy. A useful guide for anyone searching for answers and a great companion to the work of a couple's therapist." —**Eli Coleman, PhD**, academic chair in sexual health, professor, and director of Institute for Sexual and Gender Health at University of Minnesota Medical School

"Relationships—even the most excellent ones—are often messy with maladies, and *Relationship Rx* provides practical, proven, and insightful support from renowned specialists to help couples live enriched lives together through thick and thin. Based on real-world common couple challenges, this book provides use-it-today guidance to help relationships in all stages of development be more fulfilling, sustainable, and alive. It is a resource I recommend to all my patients who are looking to improve intimacy and connection in their relationship." —**Serena McKenzie, ND, IF, NCMP**, founder of Whole Life Medicine, specialist in sexual medicine

RELATIONSHIP Rx

PRESCRIPTIONS FOR LASTING LOVE AND DEEPER CONNECTION

Jessica Griffin, PsyD, and Pepper Schwartz, PhD

ROWMAN & LITTLEFIELD
Lanham • Boulder • New York • London

Published by Rowman & Littlefield
An imprint of The Rowman & Littlefield Publishing Group, Inc.
4501 Forbes Boulevard, Suite 200, Lanham, Maryland 20706
www.rowman.com

86-90 Paul Street, London EC2A 4NE

Distributed by NATIONAL BOOK NETWORK

British Library Cataloguing in Publication Information Available

Library of Congress Cataloging-in-Publication Data

Names: Griffin, Jessica, 1977– author. | Schwartz, Pepper, author.
Title: Relationship Rx : prescriptions for lasting love and deeper
  connection / Jessica Griffin and Pepper Schwartz.
Description: Lanham : Rowman & Littlefield Publishing, [2023] | Includes
  bibliographical references and index. | Summary: "This book is for
  couples with worrisome—even painful—issues, who are willing to work to
  change. The authors suggest relationship 'prescriptions' for everything
  from teensy to terrible relationship issues, to return struggling
  relationships back to health"— Provided by publisher.
Identifiers: LCCN 2022025365 (print) | LCCN 2022025366 (ebook) | ISBN
  9781538165737 (cloth) | ISBN 9781538165744 (epub)
Subjects: LCSH: Couples—Psychology. | Relationship quality.
Classification: LCC HQ801 .G747 2023 (print) | LCC HQ801 (ebook) | DDC
  306.7—dc23/eng/20220613
LC record available at https://lccn.loc.gov/2022025365
LC ebook record available at https://lccn.loc.gov/2022025366

JG: To my children, Carter, Delaney, and Jack, who, from their first breath, have taught me a kind of love I could not begin to describe and for whom I try every day to make the world a little better. And to my husband, Jon, for letting me bounce ideas and relationship exercises off him (without complaining!) and who is, and always will be, my happy place.

PS: To my husband Fred, who so generously donates some of our time together to the time I spend devoted to writing and thinking about relationships in general.

CONTENTS

CONTENTS

INTRODUCTION

The couple, Jaxson and Rachel, looked at anything but one another. At the beginning of their session, they said they loved each other, but their grimaces, awkward silences, and occasional jabs tossed back and forth told another story. Jaxson said Rachel let their fifteen-year-old insult him without correction and that she would rather be with their children than with him. Rachel questioned why Jaxson said he loved her when there was nothing but constant criticism about how she looked, her weight gain, her parenting, and her "mood swings," noting that she has struggled with bouts of depression. Rachel got ready to go on with the list of complaints he had about her, and then she sighed, thinking about how long the list of disparaging remarks actually was. She was trying, she said, to remember anything nice he had said to her in a long time—outside of when he proclaimed his love in therapy, not to her, but to the therapist when he said, "Of course I love my wife." Jaxson said it was hard to say anything positive about Rachel when she "doesn't treat me like a husband, just a guy who pays the bills and mows the lawn," and claimed that she refuses to be sexually intimate with him and "barely touches me anymore." Rachel said that when it came to sex, she was "tired of being an outlet instead of a person" and "there's nothing about him that makes me want to have sex with him lately."

If you just took a snapshot of this couple, you might think they were doomed. Their demeanor, their nasty remarks, Rachel's depression, and the lack of physical or sexual intimacy made it seem like they were at the end of what has been their relationship's long downward slide. But if you sat through their entire session, not just the snippet we told you about, you'd find a much more hopeful situation. Despite the unhappiness, there were clear signs that no one was going anywhere—there was still a heartbeat for this marriage. Jaxson and Rachel said they didn't want to get divorced—they thought they were "perfect for each other"—but they each also admitted to being extremely unhappy. There was the paradox: They still believed that the reasons they had become a couple were good ones and that they had a lot in common. But they could not find a way to be nice to each other anymore. They tended to stay away from each other even during the precious little private time they had after work and raising their kids, and they were both feeling hurt, angry, and deprived. They lived parallel lives most of the time and didn't talk much except at family dinner—when they actually had one—and during emotional flare-ups that occasionally turned into all-out warfare in the home.

Jaxson and Rachel's marriage looked pretty unhealthy—it was unhappy, unappetizing, and unpromising. Except for one thing: they really didn't want to stay that way. So even though they didn't think it would do much good, they sought help from a professional. And you know what? That was really all it took. By declaring themselves "a hot mess" and acknowledging that their relationship had become unhealthy, they allowed someone to give them the Relationship Medicine they needed in order to get better. They faced their issues, excavated the deeper reasons for their hurt and angry feelings, and in fact did get happier, kinder, and back into bed (and we don't mean to sleep!). Their marriage went from infirmed to having its health restored. The key: They not only said they *wanted* to change but also really did *work* to change.

So how do we help *you*?

This book is for couples with worrisome—even painful—issues who are willing to work to change. It is also a book for couples who are having smaller issues that are minor now but portend real problems in the future if they aren't addressed. What we do is suggest relationship "prescriptions" for everything from teensy to terrible relationship issues to return struggling relationships back to health.

We know relationships can be amazingly resilient—so if you are overwhelmed, disheartened, or even depressed about the two of you right now, take heart. Even some of the toughest stuff can be fixed with the right techniques, supports, or interventions. We have Relationship Prescriptions that can address even the most troubling of romantic relationship wounds and woes.

Let's be clear who we are talking about here because this is a really big group of people. Having serious issues, or characteristics that are less than healthy, in a relationship is not rare. Most couples, if they compiled a wish list for changes they'd like to make to their relationship, would have at least a few big items to put on that list. In fact, think about this: Ask almost anyone you know to list off some model couples, people whose relationships they truly envy—who they think are #relationshipgoals. They might know one or two couples who inspire them, but if they also knew the behind-the-scenes truths of what those couples have gone through or the compromises they have had to make, they would likely change their minds and decide that those couples aren't ones to aspire to be like at all!

The reality is that relationships are messy—that's why there are armies of therapists, counselors, coaches, and clinicians who work full time meeting the needs of troubled couples. And while there are enrichment classes that help great couples get greater, for most couples, the only time they want help is when the relationship is in trouble and one or both partners are in pain. On average, couples wait six years after issues have arisen to seek intervention to improve or save their marriages. Unfortunately, by this time, resentment has built, patterns are entrenched, and ultimately the majority of these marriages end in divorce. Often, the therapist is called in to resuscitate a marriage that is gasping for air—and may have taken its last breath. These are some of the most difficult situations to navigate as a therapy professional.

It doesn't take a PhD to realize that maybe it would be better to solve relationship problems before there is that critical lack of oxygen—that if couples were equipped with the knowledge and the tools (in the form of Relationship Vitamins or Medicine), they could prevent their relationships from running out of air.

Although an online connection or a "swipe right" is easy, long-term love in the form of healthy relationships isn't easy. Time goes by and jobs, kids, and life get in the way before a couple realizes they are both miserable or no longer in the relationship or marriage they want. Research repeatedly demonstrates that long-lasting relationships are the key to better health, wealth, and longevity and even a better sex life. Yet one look at the data suggests that we are far from this kind of utopia. The statistics are daunting. Couples are struggling. Men and women in their thirties feel the pressure to get married and have families while they are still young. The only problem is they can't find the right relationship or believe that they have to settle when they do. Meanwhile, divorce rates for first marriages continue to hover around 50 percent. So many people over age forty have had marriages that ended in divorce, and yet those people continue to look for love, determined not to make the same mistakes they made in their first marriages. And even older people are not safely situated. The divorce rate for people over age fifty (these are people in twenty-five-, thirty-five-, and even fifty-year marriages) is record high.

We believe that if these couples had simple, evidence-based tools and strategies to improve their communication and relationships—in the form of Relationship Vitamins, Medicine, or even CPR—not only would many of these marriages not end in divorce, but those couples would also be much happier and healthier together.

But let us be clear: This isn't a book of false hope. Rather, this is a book of marriage-saving advice and exercises that can be implemented, just like you take your daily vitamins or even antibiotics when you're sick, without expensive therapeutic interventions.

In this book, you will be shown how to do the following:

- Use decades of science and research on relationships, adult attachment, healthy versus unhealthy communication patterns, and evidence-based cognitive behavioral therapy techniques to your advantage.
- Make small changes to your daily life and your communication patterns.
- Discover how your past relationship trauma may be impacting your present.
- Identify blind spots or potential viruses in your relationships.

- Use simple daily Relationship Vitamins or Relationship Medicine to prevent or cure problems that are plaguing your relationships.

By making small adjustments, you and your partner will be able to vastly deepen your connection and improve your relationship's immune system so you can withstand life stressors and vastly improve your well-being and overall happiness.

Today we have the paradox of demanding more of our relationships at precisely the moment when we have less to give our partners. Dr. Eli Finkel and his coauthors captured this situation perfectly in a memorable article called "Climbing Mount Maslow" in the book *The Suffocation of Marriage: Climbing Mount Maslow Without Enough Oxygen* (2014). What Finkel and others focused on was how Dr. Abraham Maslow, a famous psychologist, had put together a theory that humans have a series of needs that start with survival (food, shelter, etc.). If those survival needs are satisfied, humans proceed to satisfy more psychological and emotional needs. At the top of this pyramid of needs is the highest level of communion with another human being—having what society tends to refer to as a "soul mate" (that is, one's life partner). What Finkel et al. note, however, is that we aspire to this pinnacle of emotional achievement at precisely the time when we are working more hours to satisfy expensive living conditions, having kids without an extended family to help out, and having our spare time taken up with technical distractions like Zoom, TikTok, Netflix, and our smartphones, so we are destined to fall short of our romantic expectations of what marriage and/or love should be like. We are set up for disappointment.

Don't get us wrong. We are hardly suggesting everyone give up hopes of romantic love and instead become Buddhist monks. What we *are* saying is that the achievement of a fulfilling relationship is no small feat, and if people are going to come even close to what they want, they need help. We understand that *many people can feel so overwhelmed that they are dispirited and feel all is lost. That is totally understandable. But we are here to give hope and help.*

Of course, psychologists and other kinds of clinicians know about helping couples—that's what they are trained to do. But the fact is we also know that not everyone who needs help has the time—or the financial resources—to commit to improving their relationships during numerous fifty-minute sessions with professionals.

Understanding that dilemma, many experts (ourselves included) have turned to producing research papers, books, articles, podcasts, social media blasts, and even reality television shows about relationships and as many kinds of outreach as we can think of in order to be of some use to people who need to be happier together but, for a lot of different reasons, cannot go to therapy or be in therapy long enough to resolve their issues. We believe there have to be other ways of reaching people because we know that for many—maybe even most—couples, important and beneficial changes can happen if we can give people tools for self-reflection, a path for self-discovery, and clear and kind methods for resolving disputes or negotiating change. As behavioral science professionals, we believe our training, research, decades of experience, and unique observation and knowledge of couples (even in the reality-television-show world!) give us excellent tools to help relationships heal, grow, and thrive.

Like other experts who study and work with couples, we know that compatible characteristics are not enough to sustain a marriage—life throws challenges at couples almost as soon as they meet, and more keep coming through the years. Most couples who end up in long-term relationships go from a honeymoon stage and various degrees of a "hot and heavy" stage to the practicalities and issues of everyday life. They must tackle changes in luck, looks, family responsibilities, budgets, sexual interest, health, and even their hopes and dreams. We have seen couples get so frustrated and overwhelmed by changes they did not expect or want that they stop trying to help their marriages get back to their original happiness, and they even stop trying to come to terms with the fact that happiness looks different now—not worse, just different.

Yes, we can help.

While no one is a relationship shaman, we think the general public underestimates what a good counselor or therapist can do—even when a couple has serious problems. Dr. Jessica is a licensed clinical and forensic psychologist with enormous clinical and research experience. She has a thriving private practice and is the leader of a statewide trauma center and a national center on relationships in the University of Massachusetts Chan Medical School Department of Psychiatry. She has studied and developed programs, services, studies, and supports related to attachment, relationships, and trauma for over two decades. Dr. Pepper, with a PhD in sociology and as a professor at the University of Washington, has a fifty-year career of creating research and understanding about love and all kinds of relationships. For almost nine years, she has been involved in helping to create and sustain marriages on a national television show. Dr. Jessica was also part of that effort, having worked on television shows in which couples turned to drastic social experiments to save their marriages. In fact, the two of us met as relationship experts on a reality television show about romantic relationships and marriage. In our many late nights and early mornings together talking about all things related to couples, it occurred to us that there are so many tools and techniques we have that could benefit other couples—even those who don't necessarily want to sign up for reality TV. On one of these late nights, Dr. Jessica said to Dr. Pepper, "I just want to write all couples prescriptions for their relationships—to prevent some of the disasters we keep seeing and to prevent the pain that results. If we could just take our Relationship Vitamins, or even Medicine, when the relationship is less than healthy and prevent long-term dire consequences—wouldn't that be a good thing?" And so this book was born.

We both have the background necessary to transform a troubled relationship into a happy and stable partnership. No, we are not magicians, but most of the time magic is not required. All that is needed is the desire of both partners in a relationship to save that relationship, to be coachable (i.e., willing to take in our insights and try them out), and to hold themselves accountable to the process. When couples do this, truly remarkable things can happen.

In this book, you will find a series of practical guides and tools grounded in relationship science that can help you and your partner take on tough issues and solve them—or at least get to a point where you no longer undermine the relationship. Each chapter highlights a common problem that couples may face (and if you haven't faced it yet, chances are you will!) and introduces three couples (case studies based on couples from our work doing private counseling, coaching, and workshops) illustrating different levels of threat to the relationship. At the Relationship Vitamins level, you will meet a couple with mild relationship issues who are reasonably happy but could benefit from taking their "vitamins" to strengthen their connection and be even happier. At the Relationship Medicine level, you'll meet a couple that is struggling and in pain—with varying degrees of unhappiness or resentment. This couple would benefit from a more intense "dose" of relationship exercises or strategies in order to restore them to health. Finally, at the Relationship CPR level, you'll meet a couple that is truly in crisis—those who many marital therapists may think are doomed without intervention. We'll suggest how to work with professionals and how to tease out the issues so that the professional intervention may be successful. Each chapter will conclude with straightforward, practical exercises that can change a downward spiral into a more aware, intimate, and thriving partnership. Our list of issues (clearly stated in the table of contents at the beginning of this book) includes the most common ones that have come before us—and those you may have experienced. And although this is a long list, it should be encouraging to know that the record shows these challenges can be taken on and defeated even when, at first glance, it looks impossible. We fully believe we can help your marriage or relationship improve before you have to do something drastic, like go on a reality television show or give it Relationship CPR. The process won't always be easy, but it will be rewarding. Let's get started.

1

FEAR OF CHANGE

I'm never going to change. Why is he so different now? This is not what I imagined our marriage to be. She was never this boring when we were dating. I thought we were on the same page about what we wanted. Don't ever let someone change who you are.

"Nobody will change me." There is no bigger, or more common, problem for a marriage than resisting or refusing change. Yet it is totally understandable—change, or even considering change, messes with our established habits or treasured ways of thinking. It can be a subtle or not-so-subtle criticism of the present—and the need to change is often resisted because it seems like admitting some sort of defect, that we aren't good enough. Plus, people love their habits so much that often failure to change isn't seen as a problem at all. In fact, standing one's ground, *no matter what*, is often seen as admirable, something for one to be proud of. Yet without change, there is no growth.

Dr. Pepper once saw a very interesting experiment that told her how much people can dislike change—even if it is occasioned by nothing particularly important and requires very little energy or thought. She was at a conference that invited one of the authors of the book *Leadership and the One Minute Manager*,[1] and so she, among others, had come to the small conference room a bit early to get a good seat. When the speaker arrived, the room was filled. He introduced himself and then told everyone they had to move to the opposite side of the room they were on. People grumbled and were definitely put out. But they did it. When the dust settled, Spencer Johnson, MD, looked at everyone and said, "Look at how ticked off you got about a very minimal change to what you had planned, and it was a change with very little consequential loss of place or time. How are you going to handle change when it really has consequences?"

So, we don't like change in general—and some people are phobic about it. They like themselves the way they are, and it's your problem if you don't. But resistance to change is everyone's problem because life and relationships require change—they require that we adjust to shifting circumstances. Consider these kinds of situations: a spouse loses a job and wants to change cities; a partner who was a superior athlete and a great jogging partner develops spine problems and can no longer run; a couple has a child with an intellectual disability requiring more of their time and attention than they had anticipated. All these cause a change of plans—or a reset on expectations for what you had envisioned life looking like—but they aren't even the hardest kind of change. The hardest kind is when you or your partner needs to change behavior that affects both of you. When one or both partners refuse to even consider change, it can create a crisis—even in very long-term marriages. We know of what we speak, and not only as professionals. We have both been in marriages that went through the good times—and the bad—and those marriages required major adjustments. Not just once but again and again, over time.

Lillian Hellman, the novelist, once wrote that "people change and forget to tell each other." Yes, change can sneak up on you—even if the seeds of change have been germinating for a long time. Bottom line: People do change, and even if it's only one member of the couple who sees oneself or his or her partner in a new way or is no longer willing to tolerate old behaviors, change is going to be required. And here's the truth: Just one person changing disrupts the marital or family system. If even the idea of change is resisted, the sleeping giant of resentment may awaken, and fierce encounters become inevitable.

Let's look at three couples, and we will, as we do in each chapter, focus on a first couple that has some *mild* relationship symptoms for which we can provide some easily done, effective exercises that will help the couple work their way out of an issue; a second couple with *moderate* relationship symptoms that needs serious help; and finally a third couple with *severe* relationship symptoms—in other words, the couple is in big trouble and will definitely need professional intervention. Each couple needs a different Relationship Prescription: The first couple needs their Relationship Vitamins, the second warrants Relationship Medicine, and the third requires Relationship CPR in the form of professional intervention when there is a true crisis that warrants intensive intervention or the relationship will end.

Couple #1: Francisco and Abby: Mild Relationship Symptoms Related to Fear of Change

Francisco and Abby are in their late twenties and are planning to get married, but they come from different religious traditions with equally opinionated, strong-willed parents vigorously opposed to a marriage outside their own families' religious traditions. Neither Francisco nor Abby wants to upset their parents, so they have been pretending to each set of parents that they are honoring that family's religious traditions. Now, facing a wedding date, Francisco is suddenly much more insistent on a Catholic ceremony, and Abby thought they had compromised on a Unitarian minister. Francisco is saying he cannot do that, as it would "break my parents' hearts." Abby, who comes from a nonreligious Jewish background, is feeling upset because Francisco had said he could be happy with a Unitarian ceremony and now he is saying he just can't change for his parents' sake. Abby is wondering just how rigid and traditional Francisco will be in the future if he is unable to make this change with her.

Couple #2: Monika and Kareem: Moderate Relationship Symptoms Related to Fear of Change

Monika and Kareem, both age forty-eight, were high school sweethearts who married in college under the presumption that she would travel with him no matter where his career demanded he go. Now she wants to change the deal, but he is sticking to their original "contract." She has become much more serious about her career over the years—and she thought Kareem knew that. But Kareem is counting on pursuing his career at the highest level and feels that Monika is changing the rules that they both originally accepted. Resentment is building on both sides, and they aren't as happy as they used to be.

Couple #3: Heidi and Dan: Severe Relationship Symptoms Related to Fear of Change

Heidi and Dan have been married fifteen years, and their relationship is full of recriminations, blowups, and insults. They used to be inseparable, but that has all changed. When Dan gets mad at her, he uses terrible language and yells at the top of his voice. She has told him she is willing to hear him out but not when he is disrespectful and threatening. Dan says he is who he is, having grown up in a "tough neighborhood" where fighting was a sport. He explained that everyone in his family yelled and used rough language and that she should just accept his blowups—he has always been hotheaded, so why should he change? They have even gone to counseling, but Dan does the same thing whenever they have a fight. He feels like Heidi has "gone soft" and that she "isn't the same woman I married—she doesn't appreciate me for who I am." Nothing gets resolved, and they are both fed up with each other. Dan has refused to go back to counseling, and Heidi is talking to a lawyer.

All three of these couples—though at different stages and levels of severity in their relationships—have one thing in common: At the core of their issues is a resistance or refusal to change.

This resistance to change isn't anyone's fault. It's biology, baby! In fact, we are hardwired to resist change. Our brains prefer routine and to be in control—habits and routines can send signals of safety to our brains that all is right in the world.[2] Getting outside our comfort zones when things are uncertain sends strong signals to the limbic system of the brain, triggering a heightened alarm system, which can feel unpleasant or uncomfortable. Research has demonstrated that uncertainty, which is inevitable if we are considering change, can actually be more stressful to us than knowing for sure that there will be negative consequences![3] So, we hold tight to our comfy habits, even if they aren't helping us or our relationships. We do want to make a distinction here that we are not talking about a diagnosable phobia, in which fear of change is so extreme that it's debilitating (e.g., you can't leave your house or take care of yourself or your kids). That is called metathesiophobia, and it requires professional intervention.

Let's take a closer look at our couples.

Francisco and Abby: Mild Relationship Symptoms in Need of Relationship Vitamins

Francisco and Abby have been having trouble creating their own independent household spirituality and religious practices, have experienced pressure from each of their families not to change their beliefs or customs, and have resisted making any changes or decisions—and it's stressing them out!

Francisco and Abby fell in love in college. They met at a party during their sophomore year, and they found each other attractive and fascinating. They are from very different cultures, but in the beginning that just added to their mutual fascination. Abby comes from a middle-class Jewish background, and Francisco comes from a well-off Catholic family of Mexican descent. They knew that their families would not be keen on this pairing for religious reasons (Abby's family is Jewish and observant; Francisco's family is Catholic, and while not devout, they go to church for more than just special holidays). The couple initially handled their differences by not mentioning each other to their families, just telling them that they were "dating around." But after graduation, Francisco proposed to Abby and she accepted; both knew, of course, that now their relationship would have to be revealed. Since neither of them was particularly religious, they settled on the idea of joining a Unitarian church and having what they felt would be a nondenominational ceremony.

When they each told their families about the compromise, their families reacted angrily. Abby was told that she would be ruining thousands of years of cultural and family tradition, and her family predicted that she would be raising children in the Catholic faith, which made her parents very unhappy. Francisco's mother cried and told him that she and his father were arranging for him to meet lovely and "moral" women and that he was "settling" and "too young to know what he was doing." Both families held their ground. Visits to each did not give Francisco and Abby reassurance that they could solve this issue. Each family wanted possible grandchildren to be raised in its own faith, and while neither family was rude to the other partner, they were not warm either.

This long-expected reaction unexpectedly shook Francisco and Abby up. Family is important to them, and the vision of real family opposition unsettled their plans. Coming in for counseling, Abby talked nonstop about never wanting to hurt her mother and her very religious brother. Francisco, deeply in love with Abby, put his head in his hands and didn't see a way forward—but he also didn't want to lose Abby. Both were steeped in his or her family's idea of tradition, and they knew that if they married, major changes would be required. They were frightened about failing or disappointing their families and each other, both in the present and in the future. And truth be told, they were terrified of change. They had picked the Unitarian church as a compromise, but, quite honestly, they didn't know that much about it. While they had not been really that observant of their religions, they were culturally comfortable with family traditions during holidays such as Hanukkah, Yom Kippur, Christmas, and Easter. They had not thought about how being Unitarian would configure their religious or nonreligious household.

Abby and Francisco had to find out whether their relationship was strong enough to deal with change (that was met with continued parental resistance) or whether they lacked the ability to accept the other person's religion enough to satisfy their parents. Francisco got especially freaked out and just wanted to end the dramatic climate that had now entered their previously happy relationship. He felt he had been too hasty, and when he went to a Unitarian service, it seemed foreign to him. He wanted to back out of his deal with Abby, but when she erupted about his change of heart, he became torn about what to do. Seeing his strong backlash against a change they were making together, Abby felt their pending marriage and potential family were endangered.

Monika and Kareem: Moderate Relationship Symptoms in Need of Relationship Medicine

Monika and her husband, Kareem, came for help because Kareem wanted to move to another state, and Monika felt that for more than ten years everything had been on his terms and she was "tired of it being all about Kareem." It was a fair complaint. Kareem's job required moves every three years, and Monika wanted to finally stay put in their home she had grown to love in

Illinois. But Kareem was being offered a major promotion—overseas in London—and it would only happen if they moved.

The dialogue between them could be reduced to this:

Monika: "I don't want to lose all my friends again. I don't want to yank the kids out of school again. I have created and sold three homes in less than twelve years. I have been 'the good corporate wife.' But I miss my old community and it was hard to establish one here. I am done. If you want to go, fine. But you're going without me and we can figure out a long-distance marriage."

Kareem: "Our lifestyle is dependent on my job. You knew this when you said 'I do.' We discussed this thoroughly and you even thought it was going to be adventurous and exciting. And we weren't kids when we talked about this. I had finished business school, and we knew what this career would look like. We decided that we would do one job and you could have your wish to be there for the kids. You could stay at home because of my job. This new position will set us up for the future. I know it's hard, but it's the deal we made."

It's easy to see each person's position. There is no right or wrong here. Monika had moved a lot and she wanted to put down roots—for at least a while. Kareem had done what he said he would do, which was support the family, and he had an opportunity to do an even better job of it. What's the answer?

Well, it all depends on whether you think feelings, opinions, needs, and priorities can change over a lifetime. Kareem didn't think they could—he was thinking like the business-minded person he was. A "deal" was made, and in his world, you stick with the deal. But Monika didn't fully comprehend what that transaction would feel like after more than twenty years. She didn't know what it would feel like for that long—she had only an *idea* of what it would feel like. It was fine when the kids were small; her priority was her kids and their future, so the moves, not easy at any time, still seemed worthwhile. But the accumulated wear and tear of setting up a home, then selling it, establishing a new home, and then selling it and managing new schools for the kids, new community contacts, and so on, wore on her. In addition, she had put her own passions on the back burner—she worked from home as a writer, mostly for popular health magazines, but she wanted to be able to focus her attention on other writing projects. Her husband had always made the lion's share of their income, because she had focused more on caring for their family, and her work had always come second. She wanted a new deal, but Kareem wanted to keep the old one. Furthermore, the old deal promised much more economic reward than at any time in the past. He felt he, and the family, could not financially afford to miss this chance.

The big problem here was that Kareem didn't want to change his upward climb to what he perceived as success, while Monika was craving stability, familiarity, and a coherent life. She had changed her life and place many times for Kareem, but Kareem, though understanding this process was hard on Monika, still wanted to invoke their original promise to each other. In his mind, it was an unending contract. Monika talked about how she was afraid to make new friends and connections, and she talked about how painful it had been for her to feel so lonely in prior moves. She said that she felt worried and anxious about potential disruptions for the kids now that they were at an age when continuity mattered and their social networks were growing. She talked about her past and promises she had made to herself that she would have a "real home" when she was an adult, and now she thought she was in the same situation again. Lastly, she expressed a deep sadness to Kareem and said, "I'm afraid you don't love me anymore."

Kareem said he does love Monika, but he had always wanted to prove to himself that he could be respected and be a great provider for her and their family. He didn't really know who he would be if he didn't achieve in his job. He knew it was hard on her and the kids, and he hated that, but he felt like this next step was the "big" one, and if he didn't do it, he would regret it forever. He then acknowledged feeling a bit insecure, and as he was getting older, he worried he was losing his grip at work, watching others junior to him get promoted while he had been patient.

Chances are that Kareem and Monika, with effective communication and some effort, could work through this impasse in a way in which they compromise for each other. Compromises could include the following: He would not go and instead look for a job that did not require a move but was an equivalent "promotion"; she would stay, and he would go for only a year with a promise to come back; they would commute back and forth as a family; or she would go and this would be the last time. If they could not come up with a compromise and Kareem wanted to go and she refused, then it would be time for Relationship CPR in the form of seeing a couples therapist because the marriage likely would be on the verge of ending. In therapy, they could focus on whether the marriage was worth saving to them, how to best negotiate resentment regarding Kareem's choice to move and Monika's choice to stay, and how to best support their children.

Heidi and Dan: Severe Relationship Symptoms in Need of Relationship CPR

Heidi and Dan had a tempestuous relationship from day one. But still, they had been together for fifteen years of marriage, so there was a strong tie that kept them together.

Since they had children, Heidi had borne the bulk of the parenting responsibilities as she worked from home maintaining a small but successful business selling her watercolors. Their sons were now preteens. Dan owned a dentistry practice, worked long hours but adored his kids, did not believe in divorce, and in any case was very physically attracted to his wife, as she was to him. But when Dan got mad, he was out of control. He felt that Heidi should understand that he would apologize later, but the way he acted was the way he blew off steam and he couldn't change, saying, "It's in my blood." He felt she should know that if he called her names and screamed at her, he would feel bad later, and she should just understand and wait and know that he would never hurt her. In fact, he was angry that she would intimate that he would do such a thing.

Dan was a rigid guy who wanted things on his own terms, and every time Heidi wanted a change, he came back in full resistance mode and said hurtful and often vulgar words. For example, although he made an exceptionally good living and they lived in an expensive suburb, he got furious when she wanted a new car or an expensive vacation. He had called her ugly names—some we are not going to print here. But quite regularly, those terms included "crazy," "stupid," "spoiled," "old," and "manipulative," and when he drank, they were a lot worse. He had been spending more and more time at the bar down the street—he said just to decompress after work without being "nagged" by Heidi. She wanted the name-calling and explosive reactions to stop, and he said that she made too big a deal about his behavior and that it was "just the way I am." Heidi had been seeing a therapist privately to vent her anger and hurt and to figure out whether she could stay in the marriage. She admitted to the therapist that she felt lonely and unloved, and even though she and Dan had a passionate sex life, she had been flirting with men online because she just wanted some man to tell her something nice about herself. She felt that she could not take any more abuse and found herself creating emotional affairs with men she interacted with through selling her artwork.

RELATIONSHIP Rx FOR EACH COUPLE

Couple: Francisco and Abby

Prescription: Relationship Vitamins: "Your Problem SOLVED" Strategy Problem

Problem-solving strategies, borrowed from cognitive behavioral therapy principles, are effective ways to help individuals and couples feel unstuck or less overwhelmed by a problem. The "Your Problem SOLVED" strategy is an exercise that Dr. Jessica developed and utilizes in couples-coaching sessions and in her online courses.[4] The point of this exercise is to take yourself out of what you have been doing because, let's face it, that just hasn't been working or isn't working well—even if what you've been doing is avoiding the problem. Instead, you do something in a way you haven't done before. A major goal of this exercise is to help individuals and couples get unstuck from problems and realize there are things (often many things) they can do about their problems. On your own and then together, you can brainstorm potential solutions.

First, **state** the problem clearly. Try to describe the problem in two to three sentences and identify what about this issue makes it a problem for you. Ask yourself: What feelings does this problem bring up for me? How is this problem getting in the way of our relationship? Discuss, as matter-of-factly as you can, the impact of this problem on your lives and relationship.

Second, **outline** your goals for solving the problem. What do you want to accomplish in solving this problem? How do you want to feel once you solve this problem? How will your relationship look when this problem is solved?

Third (and this is the part that takes the most work), **list** any and all possible solutions, even bad ideas. You also want to make sure you always include "do nothing" because chances are, you've been doing that. By putting "do nothing" on the list, you now can make a conscious decision to do nothing rather than avoid the problem based strictly on your own anxious "freeze" response.

Fourth, **verbalize**—talk through a possible plan with your partner using one or a combination of more than one possible solution on your list that feels the most comfortable. Sometimes, if all the solutions are pretty uncomfortable, it may help to ask each other, "What is the least bad solution?" and start there.

Fifth, **execute** your plan and follow through with it, encouraging each other along the way.

Finally, **determine** the outcome (successful or not?) and discuss this result with your partner. If you think your chosen solution was not successful, that's OK—you can go back to your list, even generate new solutions, and try a different strategy.

- S: State the problem clearly.
- O: Outline your goal for solving the problem.
- L: List possible solutions, even bad ones.
- V: Verbalize the plan using one or a combination of possible solutions.
- E: Execute the plan.
- D: Determine the outcome and, if not successful, try different solutions.

So, in this instance, Abby and Francisco went back to their commitment to each other and how important that was. In other words, they remembered that they wanted to be together and they wanted to create a new religious tradition between them that still showed respect for the traditions they grew up with. Francisco had to examine why he was wavering in his decision. Was he afraid of change? Did his religion mean much more to him than he realized? Or was he just a son who hated to deeply disappoint his parents? The exercise essentially was a brainstorming session of listing all the potential solutions, even bad ideas, to how Francisco felt, what he really wanted for the long run of the marriage, what Abby wanted and why, and also how their families' reactions affected their wedding plans. The two of them would be laying everything out between them and tackling the problem together. For example, Abby said, "What if we could have a civil ceremony, or what if we got married twice—once in each faith? Or, in the future, what if we could do a ceremony for each child at birth that celebrates each of their ancestries?" They could see whether they really wanted to create a totally different spiritual life in the Unitarian church—or not, if Francisco didn't truly feel comfortable there. They could investigate another approach—say, the local Ethical Society, another group that recognizes the value of all religions but practices none in a traditional manner. Could that make them feel like a strong, spiritual family? Or, as many couples do, could they educate their children on both their religious traditions? Could they have a plan to present to their respective families that was so solid that their families would eventually accept the fact that Francisco and Abby had their own spiritual plan?

Abby and Francisco came up with a list together and included even solutions that were distasteful to each of them. They came up with a strategy they felt comfortable with and enacted their plan, and while it was bumpy at first, they were surprised at how soon their respective families accepted their approach. Moreover, Francisco felt that he grew as a person by challenging himself about facing change and facing his family as an adult man who was going to be able to act independently from his relatives.

FRANCISCO AND ABBY'S PROBLEM SOLVED WORKSHEET

S: STATE THE PROBLEM CLEARLY

Our families are putting pressure on us to each follow our family's religious traditions and practices. We are afraid to upset our families and upset each other. We are afraid to make a decision that results in a change that further strains our marriage and our relationships with our families.

O: OUTLINE YOUR GOAL FOR SOLVING THE PROBLEM

We want to decrease the stress related to this problem and come to an agreement so that this problem does not affect our relationship and we have a solution we are happy with.

L: LIST POSSIBLE SOLUTIONS, EVEN BAD ONES

- Do nothing.
- Abby converts to Catholicism.
- Francisco converts to Judaism.
- Stop speaking to family.
- No longer practice any religion.
- Research what other couples who have been in similar situations have done.
- Go to couples therapy to get assistance.
- List what we each value about our respective religions.
- Interview family members about what they value the most and what traditions and values are most important to pass down.
- Find a church or spiritual center that is open to different religions and ways of thinking.
- Ask for a family meeting with both families.

V: VERBALIZE THE PLAN USING ONE OR A COMBINATION OF POSSIBLE SOLUTIONS

List what we each value about our respective religions, interview family members, and then ask for a family meeting with our parents after we have a plan we can present to them.

E: EXECUTE THE PLAN

We tried it and came up with a list that we felt comfortable with.

D: DETERMINE THE OUTCOME AND, IF NOT SUCCESSFUL, TRY DIFFERENT SOLUTIONS

We came up with a list of traditions we want to pass on and our vision for our future religious practices as a couple. We interviewed our family members separately and had a dinner respectful of both of our religions (with foods that are important to both cultures and a prayer in each religion) with our parents and presented our plan. It went so well—our parents bonded over their shared angst (ha ha), and we are ecstatic!

Couple: Monika and Kareem

Prescription: Relationship Medicine: The Circles of Priorities

This is a simple exercise that couples can do, first on their own and then later sharing and comparing circles to see how the time they spend each day is in sync (or out of sync) with their priorities and values. By comparing your own individual circles and then recognizing similarities or differences in your partner's, you can increase your clarity about what really matters and have a better understanding of your frustrations—and some clues for what to do about it!

Each partner should take a piece of paper and draw a big circle. You are about to create two pie charts.

In the first circle, list the most important things in your life. Using "slices" of the pie chart to indicate importance, rank the most important things in your life. So the biggest slice is the most important, and you can show its magnitude by how big the slice is. Do this for the following values: your marriage or main relationship, your kids (if you have them), your work, your faith, your hobbies (golf, tennis, chess, reading, etc.), your friends, your family, travel, your sex life, and anything else that is seriously important to you. When you are finished, take a second piece of paper, draw a circle on it, and create a pie chart based on how you live an average day. Setting aside a chunk of the circle for eight hours of sleep, show how a typical weekday is apportioned. Creating "slices" of the pie, draw how much of your day is spent doing the following:

- Cooking, cleaning, or doing home, yard, and automobile maintenance
- Shopping for food or household goods
- Feeding or maintaining pets, kids, and each other
- Scrolling or talking on the phone
- Being at work or doing work-related video or phone calls
- Talking with, teaching, or tucking in the kids or hearing them download their days
- Working out or exercising
- Talking to each other
- Cuddling or having sex
- Commuting (if it applies)
- Being with friends or neighbors

The list goes on. . . .

If you are like most of us, the way you spend your time and your priorities are probably way out of whack. One way Monika and Kareem could talk about the possible move was to see how it fit into what they said their priorities were. And if their priorities were seriously different from each other's, then they might need to take a different approach and talk through how they could negotiate their differences. They could then utilize the Reflective Listening Medicine discussed in chapter 2.

Couple: Heidi and Dan

Prescription: Relationship Medicine (in the Short Term) and Relationship CPR

Heidi and Dan are caught in an ugly cycle of strong passions—positive when they are being sexually intimate on a regular basis, and negative when Dan strikes out at Heidi when she has angered or hurt him or when he is just in a lousy mood—and Heidi no longer stands up for herself. We wish this problem weren't common, but it is. And it is very destructive: It erodes Dan's respect for Heidi, and it destroys Heidi's sense of self-worth. Further, it can destroy happiness in the marriage and each partner's happiness in general. This is a tough habit to break—on both sides. Dan has been getting away with it for so long that it seems normal to him, even comfortable, and Heidi has been taking this verbal abuse for so long that she doesn't know how to redraw boundaries and assert herself. But change here is absolutely necessary.

Relationship Medicine: Establishing Word Boundaries

For Dan and Heidi, just saying "I won't do that anymore" is long gone. So many ugly things have been said too many times. It's clear to us that Heidi and Dan need Relationship CPR. But as a holding action before this couple is able to receive the professional help they truly need, it might help to create a list of words that are not permitted. In this case, any word that demeans Heidi's intelligence, choices, looks, or forgetfulness should be included. If there is a trespass, the utterer (this would be Dan in this case) has to give $50 (or whatever amount would sting) to Heidi or watch a TV show that he doesn't care for and she does. If there is a string of words, the money can mount up. This has two purposes: to show the couple how frequent the word use is (Dan denied that initially) and to be an incentive to stop. A twist to this process can be added, but only if both parties agree: the money can be used for something that really bothers the offending partner. For example, Heidi is a Democrat and Dan is very conservative. Heidi, instead of using the money for clothes or other items she would like, can donate the money to the most liberal Democrat she can think of. This prospect definitely makes Dan hesitate, but it really is a last-ditch effort to see whether some civility can be achieved.

Relationship CPR

Individual therapy was prescribed to Dan to address his anger, and it turned out that drinking was involved in most of the extreme episodes. Individual therapy was also prescribed to Heidi to address her self-worth. And couples therapy was prescribed to address unhealthy patterns of communication and increase positive communication.

On a positive note, Dan got slightly better because of the exercise once he realized how frequent his negative language was toward his wife, and he actually was surprised by how frequent it had become. Still, he felt triggered by her (she would say things that made him feel unloved and disrespected too) and he would lose it—and, once again, a barrage of nasty statements would come pouring out of him. Although he was going to the bar less frequently than before, when he did go, he came home intoxicated and in a lousy mood. One time finally turned out to be too many, and Heidi packed up and left the house.

Even though this result might seem unavoidable to the average observer, Dan was shocked because he did love his wife and he assumed that they would go on with the cycle of his outbursts, her anger and hurt, and his remorse and that things would stay the same. When things changed, he begged for couples therapy again, and Heidi relented but stayed at her parents' house and said she would not move back unless there was real change. They went to couples therapy for a year, and Dan agreed to talk with a therapist to explore and address his anger and to undergo assessment to determine whether he needed additional intervention for his drinking. We applaud Heidi's decision to pack up and leave under these conditions because while we understand that Heidi wanted to stay in her marriage, insulting and humiliating words have no place in any kind of relationship and they can't be allowed to continue. In therapy, Dan learned anger modulation techniques to control his anger, including yoga, meditation, and regular exercise. He also learned how his abusive comments made Heidi feel and how damaging this was to their relationship. He likewise began to understand how he was using the same approach on her that his father had used on his mother—and he hated his father for that and other brutal acts. Realizing he was carrying on a conflict style he hated as a child, he tried hard to change his tone and words—and in one session broke down when he realized that his children were seeing the same pattern he grew up with. After that, Dan became more respectful, but it still wasn't perfect. He lost his temper and used nasty words, but it was more like once or twice per year compared to several times per week. This sent Dan and Heidi back into therapy for reinforcement of Heidi's right to be spoken to with respect. Dan, through couples therapy, became more aware of using positive statements and compliments toward his wife. Heidi decided that although she hated any blowups from Dan, she could handle their much-reduced frequency. After a year, Heidi felt that Dan had changed and was at least holding himself accountable. That change, while imperfect, made all the difference to her.

Summary

Whether because of our personality or our biology, we know that change isn't easy. We also know that those who say "I will never change" are dooming themselves to lives that are likely devoid of satisfaction, and when this happens in couples, it is a relationship killer. Embracing even small steps toward change utilizing strategies such as the worksheets and tools we use here, couples experiencing mild or moderate difficulties can shift their perspectives and resolve conflicts that may have become catastrophic down the road. For those with more severe issues, like Heidi and Dan, there are strategies that can stop the bleeding while awaiting the outcome of professional intervention. For couples at this level, if both parties are willing to work toward change, hope for a happy (and much healthier!) marriage is possible.

2

TRUST

Your Past Is Interfering with Your Present

I can't trust anyone. I'm so nervous when he leaves the house—will he be coming back? I wonder if my partner is cheating on me. Don't make yourself vulnerable—to anyone. Does she really have my back? Why do I still feel so uneasy and nervous in my relationship, even though I know my partner loves me? My partner cheated, and I don't think we will ever come back from this.

"I can't trust anyone." We have heard this statement from countless men and women—men and women who tell us that due to their past experiences, they find themselves unable to fully trust their partners. How many of us enter relationships guarding our hearts and protecting ourselves, only to find out we are holding ourselves back from genuine connection with others? The irony is that we're protecting ourselves from being hurt while ultimately hurting ourselves in the process. Many of us already in committed relationships may find ourselves embroiled in conflict with our partners—often stemming from issues related to trust. Mistrust has its place—when we do not trust, it's an attempt to protect ourselves from painful experiences, especially if we've been betrayed before. For those of us who have struggled with trust, we can ask ourselves, "What has my difficulty trusting protected me from?" Then ask, "What has it prevented me from having in my life?" We may find ourselves not fully opening up to our partners out of fear of being rejected by them or not fully trusting that they can handle the "real" us. We may find ourselves snooping through our partners' emails or phones, getting anxious when they "work late," or even accusing them of being with other people—when it's just not the case. Or we may be in relationships with people who have done any number of these things. You're not alone, as trust issues are commonplace—especially with the increase in the use of the Internet, smartphones, and social media and how quickly we can "connect" with other people. The majority of the time when trust is an issue for couples, it's because of what's happened in one or both partners' pasts—past romantic relationships or even past relationships in childhood. Childhood relationships form a sort of mental DNA with which, based on past experiences and the impact of those experiences on our well-being or attachment styles, we can reasonably predict certain behavioral patterns we will see in adult relationships.

First, a crash course in attachment science: Dr. Jessica has spent a large part of her career studying attachment science, which has been a growing body of research over the past thirty years. Attachment science stems from work with primates and the relationships between baby monkeys and their parents. Later, it moved to studying human infant-parent relationships and then adult romantic attachments. The research has demonstrated that we each have a primary attachment style, which can fall into a couple different categories.[1] Our attachment styles can be either secure or insecure. Fifty percent of us have a primary attachment style of "secure." Insecure attachment includes anxious (about 20 percent of us), avoidant (about 20 percent of us), and disorganized (a combination of anxious and avoidant styles—about 10 percent of us). Our primary attachment styles are influenced by a number of things, beginning with our early childhood relationships, which for many people create templates they use even into their adult relationships. But that's not the only way our attachment styles are influenced—adult relationships can affect our attachment styles as well. And research also suggests a person's attachment style can change—one out of four people will change his or her primary attachment style over time.[2]

Secure attachment is like an accordion—even if there is distance between you and your partner, you are always connected. Secure attachment provides a safe haven from predators. In today's world, these predators involve stressors on our individual lives and our relationships, such as other people who might threaten our unions. When our attachments are secure, our feelings

ATTACHMENT STYLES

Secure Attachment: Feel comfortable with intimacy, are warm and loving, and do not have major issues with trust or commitment

Anxious Attachment: Crave intimacy and yet feel preoccupied, worried,
and anxious about their relationships and worry about whether their
partners want to be with them

Avoidant Attachment: Tend to minimize closeness to the extent possible, keep their partners at more than arm's length, and see relationships as a loss of their own autonomy or independence and thus
avoid intimacy

Disorganized Attachment: A combination of anxious and avoidant
attachment styles—you never know what you're going to get

of security increase, which helps promote our emotional regulation—we're
calmer and more content. When we have that firm base in our lives in the
form of securely attached relationships, our confidence in ourselves and
others improves, and we have a solid foundation to go out and explore the
world, grow, and thrive—and have something solid to return home to.

Research has yielded a few important findings: First, people with secure
attachment styles tend to be happier and healthier and in healthier, more
satisfying, longer-lasting relationships. Second, our attachment styles can
change depending on our circumstances and stressors, and—good news
here—if we have insecure attachment styles, we can improve within the
context of relationships with people with secure attachment style. For those
with anxious attachment, not-so-good news: trust issues are particularly
problematic.[3] Third, there are scientifically backed strategies we can use to
dramatically improve our relationships, even if our primary attachments are
not secure (or our partners' are not secure).

OK, science nerds, listen up: Attachment is very much rooted in the
brain. The brain has a biological mechanism designed to protect our closest relationships, called the "attachment system," which involves the limbic
system. This attachment system is responsible for monitoring the safety and
availability of our closest attachment figures, whether parents or a romantic
partner. The brain's attachment system consists of emotions and behaviors

that ensure we remain safe and protected by staying close to our loved ones. This attachment system is also responsible for protest behavior. Protest behavior could be things like, as a young child, crying frantically when separated from a parent until reunited with them or, as an adult, calling one's partner repeatedly or blowing up the partner's phone with text messages until one has a clear message that the partner (and the relationship) is safe. Within the limbic system is the amygdala, a tiny brain structure responsible for regulating our emotions and scanning for danger. The amygdala picks up on signals of threat (e.g., facial expressions, postures, voices, movements, words, and phrases). When we are under stress, the amygdala takes over and essentially hijacks the more sophisticated brain structures, like the prefrontal cortex, that are involved in tasks such as decision-making, thinking through the consequences of our actions, and problem-solving. When we are in arguments with our loved ones, our amygdalae detect the threats and, if not controlled, take over so that we are less able to effectively problem-solve issues. Essentially, our and our partners' amygdalae are duking it out and getting in the way of being able to resolve conflicts with each other. This is one of the reasons we encourage couples to take a brief break during conflict in order to allow their bodies' stress responses to diminish and their prefrontal cortexes to come back online.

When we're really worked up, there are regions of the brain that take over other areas responsible for sound decision-making, which unfortunately prevents us from being able to reason and think more abstractly and deliberately. So it's best to wait at least twenty minutes, and sometimes much longer, until this "alarm system" in the brain settles down.

When we take a look at the attachment literature, we see that trust comes from what we call a "secure base." What the heck does that mean? It means that our partners respond to us in a way that is predictable, compassionate, and available to us—that we can come to expect that our partners and our relationships with our partners are a home base for us, a soft spot to land in the world. Research has shown that if people have that secure base, they are able to form stronger connections, perform better at work, and make more money, and there are notable physical health, mental health, and longevity benefits as well.[4] And, not surprisingly, individuals with secure attachments tend to struggle far less with issues related to trust. Individuals with insecure attachment styles, such as anxious or avoidant styles, will struggle more with being able to fully trust their partners.

The good news for all of us, even if we have histories of difficulty trusting or breaches in our own current relationships, is that trust can be built or rebuilt through predictability, being compassionate toward our partners (which also involves having a better understanding of them, including their vulnerabilities), and showing up consistently for our partners. Trust also improves, as we have stronger emotional intimacy in our relationships—which we will talk about in the next chapter. But first, let's introduce three couples, all of whom struggle with some degree of trust difficulties: Adam and Justin, with mild relationship symptoms; Misha and Sam, with moderate relationship symptoms; and Duke and Dana, with severe relationship symptoms and whose marriage is on the brink of demise.

Couple #1: Adam and Justin: Mild Relationship Symptoms Related to Trust

Adam and Justin have been married for two years but together for a total of four years. Justin has been struggling with pangs of jealousy, wondering whether Adam (who is always on his phone) might be cheating. Justin has been hesitant to tell Adam about his worries and has kept this concern to himself, even avoiding Adam so he doesn't have to think about it. Adam has felt that Justin has been pulling away and has been disappointed that they haven't been spending as much time together. Neither Adam nor Justin has been direct with the other about what's been bothering them, and both are longing for increased connection with each other.

Couple #2: Misha and Sam: Moderate Relationship Symptoms Related to Trust

Misha and Sam have been together for three years, were engaged last year, and have been planning a wedding. Misha has struggled with trust issues throughout her prior relationships—avoiding committed relationships due to her own belief that she has too much baggage from her past. Sam, deeply in love with Misha, has tried to be patient with her but is starting to get impatient with her jealous behavior and outbursts, even wondering whether they should put the wedding on an indefinite hold.

Couple #3: Duke and Dana: Severe Relationship Symptoms Related to Trust

Duke and Dana have been together for thirteen years. Throughout their marriage, they have struggled with issues related to infidelity. Duke has cheated on Dana multiple times in the form of one-night stands, some known to Dana and some not. Duke claims he has sworn off one-night stands but has been spending more and more time on adult websites. Recently, Dana, fed up with years of feeling neglected and mistreated by Duke, strayed in their marriage with a former high school boyfriend. Dana and Duke have gotten to the point where neither of them really cares what the other does—they went from hurling insults to just ignoring each other. They are equally miserable.

All three of these couples are allowing their past hurts to affect their present relationships and their present levels of happiness. So you have a past. So you've been hurt before by other people. Find us someone who has never been hurt before. . . . Unless a person has never dated or has been living in a cave, it would be rare to find someone who hasn't experienced pain in the context of relationships. Some people, though, have experienced more than their fair share—from mistreatment in childhood by those who were supposed to provide care and nurturance and meet their basic needs to toxic or even abusive relationships in adulthood. So you have a relationship in which one or both of you have acted badly or in ways you aren't proud of. Find us someone who has been in a long-term relationship who hasn't—and we'll tell you they're lying. The truth is that all of us have experienced some degree of relationship harm, which, for many, may impede the ability to fully trust others, including those who are the closest to us.

What do you think the antidote to relationship harm is? Ironically, it's relationships.

Research indicates that despite the suffering we may have had in the past, it is through healthy relationships that healing can occur. Further, our relationships can serve as a buffer to stress and adversity we may encounter in the future.

Part of being able to trust means making ourselves vulnerable to a partner—exposing sides of ourselves or parts about ourselves we aren't proud of, are ashamed of, or prefer to keep secret. Trust and vulnerability make up two large components of emotional intimacy (i.e., how close and connected we feel to our partners), which we'll discuss in the next chapter. Part of being vulnerable means also sharing elements of our pasts that might potentially explain some of our present behaviors—not excuse them but explain them so that our partners may respond differently with this new knowledge in mind and/or we can figure out how to problem-solve trust issues together. Among many couples we've worked with, one or both partners often has difficulty with vulnerability and is pretty hesitant to reveal any flaws or secrets from their past out of fear that their partner might not love them in the same way or might even leave them. But think about this, those of you who have difficulty opening up and are worried that your partners will leave you if they know the "real" you: What if they never see the "real" you and they stay? Do you want to keep pretending to be someone you're not? Keeping up with the charade, keeping up with those appearances, being the person you think your partner wants but not who you really are, is downright exhausting.

Adam and Justin: Mild Relationship Symptoms Related to Trust

Lately, Justin has been feeling less secure about his relationship with Adam, noticing that Adam is preoccupied with his phone. Justin, who has struggled with body image issues and has been cheated on in his prior relationships, recently went into Adam's phone. Although he didn't find anything significant, he saw that Adam was checking on his exes' social media profiles. Justin didn't say anything but was preoccupied with what he found—he even stopped going to the gym because he started to wonder whether Adam was checking out other guys working out, and it distracted him so much from his own workout that it wasn't worth going. Adam, who has always wanted a lot of "me time," noticed that Justin hasn't seemed himself lately—he's been less interested in physical intimacy and has stopped working out with him at the gym, an activity they used to enjoy together.

In talking with Adam and Justin, one thing became clear: Neither of them has been completely honest with the other about his past or his vulnerabilities. Justin had "skimmed the surface" with Adam earlier in their relationship when he said that prior partners had cheated on him—he hadn't gotten into the extent of the cheating or the level of pain and self-doubt this situation caused. Further, he hadn't been forthcoming about his anxiety related to whether Adam was being faithful, and Adam, while he wondered what was up with Justin, hadn't been voicing his concerns about Justin pulling away. Justin has interpreted Adam's lack of noticing his pulling away as lack of interest, which fueled his insecurities. It's quite possible that their different attachment styles are contributing to some of the tension between them. The dynamic between Adam and Justin is all too common in romantic relationships—problems start brewing, but neither party voices what's really bothering him or her until it boils over and the damage has been done. Justin, in not speaking up and pulling away while he obsesses about Adam's faithfulness, is interpreted by Adam as not being as interested in him, so Adam goes about his business hoping Justin will come around. He turns his attention to his phone and the gym, and, in turn, Justin has his insecurities reinforced. Adam hasn't been open with Justin about his own past—particularly his childhood, in which he lived in a home with a highly anxious mother who was constantly doting on and hovering over him. At the same time, his father, who seemed perturbed by his mother's overinvolvement in Adam's life, as the years went on seemed to check out more and more, immersing himself in hobbies that often took him outside the home, leaving less time for Adam and the rest of the family. It's easy for us on the outside to see that if Adam and Justin were to use some simple tools or strategies *now*, they could increase their understanding of (and empathy toward) each other, increase the trust between them, and problem-solve any mild trust issues before those issues become catastrophic.

Misha and Sam: Moderate Relationship Symptoms Related to Trust

Misha first came in for a consultation. She was smart and vivacious and had quite a bit of baggage. She carried with her an abusive childhood with an alcoholic father, ongoing struggles with her weight and self-esteem, and a series of unhealthy relationships with men. Misha wore her "I'm damaged" badge equally out of honor and as an excuse—constantly blaming herself for being too damaged to love. Over time, she had enlisted the assistance of self-help gurus and trainers. No matter how fit she was or how much work she was doing on herself, Misha had kept a committed relationship off the table, engaging only in hookups with no commitment or occasional friend-with-benefits relationships. She believed there was much more work to be done on herself before she could be ready for a real relationship. Then Misha met Sam. Sam was a combination of kind and strong, with a sensitivity and resilience he had from losing his father to cancer at a young age but being supported in a loving home with his mom and grandmother. Despite Misha's multiple attempts to convince Sam early on that she was too damaged to love (e.g., getting too drunk at a party and picking a fight, being convinced that he was interested in other women and checking his email, and wondering whether he really was attracted to her or had some ulterior motive), Sam was steadfast. While he didn't support her bad behavior, he thought she was more than worthy of love. As their relationship progressed, Misha continued to engage in explosive blowups, accusing Sam of cheating on her and sometimes causing a scene. This treatment resulted in Sam changing all his passwords, withdrawing from Misha, and becoming increasingly annoyed with her behavior. He loved Misha tremendously but said, "I'm throwing my hands up. I don't know what else to do. I can't be married to someone who doesn't trust me, no matter how trustworthy I know myself to be! Why am I doing the time for someone else's crime?" Misha felt horribly guilty, hating herself after she would snoop on Sam or accuse him of cheating. She loved Sam more than any other man she had ever known. She *knew* that he loved her too, and yet she just couldn't shake her anxiety that something bad was going to happen or Sam was going to stray.

Misha had done a lot of self-improvement, had worked with a number of therapists, and had read numerous self-help books on the market, but she was getting a very unhelpful message—that her baggage needed to be resolved before she was worthy of a "real" relationship. A lot of psychologists will tell us that if we have baggage, we aren't ready for love or healthy relationships. But think about that for a minute: How many people do you know without baggage? This teaching and mindset is a myth. We don't have to have all our issues worked out before we can be loved or committed. And as we have already mentioned, it's actually through stable and nurturing relationships that the pain of past relationships can be healed. Although things have escalated between Misha and Sam, with Sam questioning whether to put their wedding on hold, both of them want to work on their relationship and have a shared goal: to create a marriage that they can both be proud of and in which they both feel safe and supported. With some techniques helping them explore how their past affects their present, Misha and Sam—and so many couples like them—can move beyond their past in a way that helps them create the future they both want.

Duke and Dana: Severe Relationship Symptoms Related to Trust

Duke and Dana's marriage has been marred by multiple affairs—Duke had engaged in a string of one-night (sometimes two-night) stands over the years, typically when he was traveling for work as a pharmaceutical rep. Around year six or seven of their marriage, Dana discovered his infidelity after she tested positive for an STD during her prenatal visits with their second child and confronted him. He claimed that this was a random occurrence, a moment of weakness at a work conference, and that he had needs that weren't fully met due to Dana's pregnancy at the time. He said that he viewed her differently now that she was the mother of his child. Focusing on the future of her family, Dana decided to bury the issue but never got over it. In the last year, Dana engaged in an emotional affair with a former high school boyfriend, which more recently became physical. At the same time, Duke had been spending hours in the late evening (and sometimes during the workday) in adult chat rooms and on online sex sites. Both Dana and Duke are miserable—in their marriage and in their individual lives. Dana says that reconnecting with her former boyfriend has made her feel alive, sexy, and wanted again. She no longer cares what Duke does. She says she is staying with Duke because she does not want her children to go through a divorce but that "there's no point in trusting someone who has repeatedly showed me he can't be trusted." Duke, appalled on discovering Dana's connection with her former boyfriend, has argued that his indiscretions are not as important because "I don't love any of those women."

All three of these couples have one thing in common: Their pasts are affecting their present relationships and their present states of well-being, whether it's their past romantic relationships in which they were cheated on, their past histories of being mistreated and abused by people who were supposed to look out for their best interests, the painful experiences of loss at a young age, the pain from partners' transgressions in the past, or the past templates from childhood that are interfering with how they behave in the present. For some, their pasts have greatly impacted their abilities to securely attach to other human beings—and they may have insecure attachments in the form of anxious, avoidant, or disorganized attachment. For others, like Duke and Dana, their pasts have wounded them in ways that make them unable to move on or forgive their partners, and they may question (and, by the way, we do as well) whether their marriages are worth saving.

So many issues people have stem from ways they were mistreated in childhood or result from not getting their needs met within the context of relationships. That can leave scars for sure. Here's the trick, though: It's actually through healthy, supportive relationships that genuine healing can begin and we can optimize our happiness. Relationships support us and sustain us and prevent stressors (past, present, or future) from becoming toxic to us—physically and emotionally.[5]

So what if you have some baggage from the past? Find us someone who doesn't. Baggage doesn't mean you aren't worthy of love, worthy of affection, worthy of forgiveness, or worthy of trust. A healthy relationship—and a relationship that fosters that secure attachment—changes everything. So many self-help books, typically geared for women, urge independence and emphasize that before there can ever be a truly healthy relationship, a person has to be "fixed," be "whole first," or "have done the work." Lying under that message is the idea that depending on someone is weak (gasp), and weakness is just plain unhealthy or anti-feminist.

We need to turn that codependency myth upside down.

Let's take a closer look at our couples to see how this process plays out.

RELATIONSHIP Rx FOR EACH COUPLE

Couple: Adam and Justin

Prescription: Relationship Vitamins: Determine Your Primary Attachment Style; Unload Your Rocks; Cognitive Triangle for Justin

Determine Your Primary Attachment Style

One of the issues that seemed readily apparent in Adam and Justin's relationship was how careful the two had been to try to preserve positive communication between them. They were afraid to bring up issues, including their own insecurities or their past wounds or histories. While their intentions to not rock the boat or upset the other person may have been solid, Adam and Justin were actually preventing themselves from increasing the closeness between them and could potentially have damaged their relationship without even knowing it. Part of being able to better understand our partners, beyond what we see on the surface, is also understanding what's beneath that—what explains some of their behaviors, fears, and quirks. A way to get a broad sketch of our partners is to explore both our own and our partners' attachment styles. There are many tools available online to assess one's primary attachment style. For a validated adult attachment questionnaire that you can take yourself, you can access the Experiences in Close Relationships–Revised (ECR-R) questionnaire at https://www.web -research-design.net/cgi-bin/crq/crq.pl.[6] For those who would like to do additional reading on the topic, an easy-to-read resource on adult attachment is the book *Attached: The New Science of Adult Attachment and How It Can Help You Find—and Keep—Love.*[7]

Justin and Adam each completed their attachment style questionnaires. Not surprisingly, Justin discovered that he had a primary attachment style of anxious, which explained the panic he would feel when he didn't hear back from Adam or when Adam was preoccupied with his phone. Adam, by contrast, had a primary attachment style of secure, although he was pretty close to avoidant. In the context of a secure attachment, Adam probably acted in a much more securely attached way—however, under stress, he tended to engage in more avoidant behavior. Both Justin and Adam, with this new revelation, were able to see how each of them might unintentionally trigger the other. As Justin discovered his attachment style, he was able to talk with Adam about his concerns that Adam seemed to be on his phone all the time and that he was feeling insecure about not just their relationship but also himself. Adam, discovering that his partner had this style, learned that Justin simply would need more reassurance, which Adam was happy to provide in the form of more regular check-ins and commenting on what he was doing on the phone. Over time, with increased reassurance, Justin settled down and his worries related to Adam's behavior decreased. He began going back to the gym with Adam, and they started planning hiking trips together, something they could both look forward to. Learning their attachment styles helped clarify a few things for both of them. Benefiting from this newfound knowledge, Adam and Justin could use another dose of Vitamins through which they learn about each other's pasts—perhaps as a way to explain their attachment styles in the present.

A Vitamins Challenge: Unload Your Rocks

Some people are not comfortable revealing secrets from their pasts, memories of moments they are not proud of, or aspects of their lives they are ashamed of. But think about it this way: Sharing these intimate details with our partners will help us unload a giant backpack of rocks. When we reveal things to our partners, they can hold these rocks for us, serving the role of what we call an "emotional container" in those moments. Then they can help us cast away these rocks, forever lightening our loads. It would be difficult for them to carry all our rocks at once, so this process happens gradually. Over time, that heavy backpack of burdens gets lighter and we're able to move through life more freely. Couples can do this exercise in two ways—draw rocks on a piece of paper, or even get outdoors and write down the information on actual rocks. Hand the rocks (whether paper or real) to your partner, and allow your partner to hold those rocks for you. At the end of the exercise, you can throw your rocks into the woods, into a pond, into the ocean—whatever works for your situation and location! On the rocks, you are to write some of the things from your past that have had a profound impact. This is a Vitamins-level exercise, as all couples could benefit from it, but we want to caution you that it may be emotional because it explores parts of your past that aren't the happiest. So do this when you're in a good headspace and make sure you reserve time for extra hugs at the end. We have some questions to get you started:

- What is one of the scariest things that has ever happened to you?
- When is a time you felt very ashamed?
- What is your first uncomfortable childhood memory?
- When is a time you felt embarrassed?
- What is a way in which you were parented that you wish you could change?
- If you could change anything about your past, what would it be?
- What is one of the saddest experiences you have gone through?
- Write about a time when you were rejected in a relationship—whether it is a friendship, family relationship, or romantic relationship.
- What has been one of your biggest regrets?
- If you could, what would you like to change about yourself?
- What's the worst thing that's ever happened to you? (If you have a long list, each one gets a rock.)
- What has been your largest barrier to accomplishing your goals in life?
- What's been your largest barrier in relationships?
- What do you not like about your body?
- What do you not like about your personality?
- What are you afraid of?

On one of their day-hiking trips, Adam and Justin decided to do this exercise—and, motivated to become closer, they took it to the next level. They collected rocks along a ravine and sat together while they each wrote their emotional load on their rocks with a marker. They each carried their rocks with them as they hiked and took turns sharing their rocks with each other throughout their trek. Justin shared his painful past of being cheated on and the things he wished he could change about his body. Adam "held" these rocks for Justin not just physically but also by offering reassurance—that he found Justin's body attractive, and that he, too, had insecurities, and that he was sorry that others had hurt Justin before. Adam also opened up about the longing he had for more time with his father growing up—and that sometimes he noticed his father in himself, diving into hobbies and work when others around him seemed anxious or stressed out. He said that he always wondered whether it was something about him that pulled his father away. Justin listened, held Adam's rocks, and offered that Adam's father missed out on some wonderful time with Adam and (knowing that Adam's father was pretty old-school) that it was more about Adam's father's inability to tolerate stressors or people talking about hard feelings that resulted in his father's avoidant behavior. In addition, Adam disclosed a history of being bullied in school for being small, by even his close friends, which he had never told Justin. Justin then understood Adam's obsession with working out—Adam turned to exercise and weight lifting as a means of protecting himself from others. At the end of their hike, they took each other's rocks, read them back to one another, and threw them into the river. After this ritual, they each felt lighter and both of them emphatically reported that they had never been closer.

By using both of these strategies, Adam and Justin had an increased understanding of each other and more compassion for each other, which translated into increased emotional (and physical!) intimacy. Of course, no strategy is perfect, and problems and conflict are inevitable—even in the healthiest and closest relationships. As issues came up for Justin and Adam, the couple could also benefit from utilizing the Reflective Listening Medicine outlined below in our discussion of our second couple, Misha and Sam. Lastly, a strategy that could greatly assist Justin with his thoughts about whether Adam would cheat on him or leave him is the Cognitive Triangle.

Cognitive Triangle

The following exercise, borrowed from cognitive behavioral therapy principles, can be used in a variety of situations to have a positive effect on our psychological well-being. Simply by changing our thoughts, as one might change a hat, we can make an impact on how we feel and what we do. Taking that one step further, we then can make an impact on how other people respond to our behavior, and we can improve our relationships.

The situation: Justin had not heard from Adam all day.

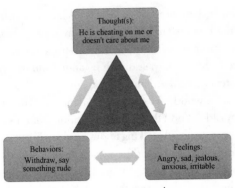

The Cognitive Triangle

Justin hadn't heard from Adam all day, even though he had reached out to him via text message. His thoughts might have been "He doesn't care about me" or "He's cheating on me" or "He's too busy to take the time to connect with me." The resulting set of feelings may have been sadness, jealousy, anger, resentfulness, irritability, or other negative emotions. If that's how Justin was feeling, his behavior might involve withdrawing from Adam, saying something rude or negative when he did see Adam, ignoring him, or withholding sex or expression of positive feelings toward him. If Justin engaged in these behaviors, Adam might become upset or angry and, as a result, withdraw or retaliate. The inevitable impact on their relationship would be that they were not brought closer together but driven further apart, which was not the outcome Justin had in mind.

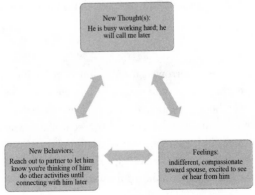

The Cognitive Triangle—Alternative Thought

The next step is to come up with an alternate thought. Imagine if Justin were to exchange this original thought with a replacement. So instead of saying "He doesn't care about me" or "He's too busy to take the time to connect with me," Justin could think, "He must be busy, and I'm sure I will hear from him later," or "His phone must have died or he's in an important meeting," or even "I do not need to hear from my spouse all day in order to be happy." Any one of these thoughts might result in a different set of feelings or behaviors. If he thought, "He must be so busy he does not have time to respond, and I'm sure I'll hear from him later," his feelings might include indifference to the situation, compassion for his spouse for his busy day, or even excitement about hearing from Adam later. Justin's behavior might be to check in at a later point to let Adam know he's thinking of him, do nothing, or engage in other activities and go about his day. This new behavior might have a neutral or even positive effect on their relationship, wouldn't result in increased conflict between them, and might even bring them closer together.

The Cognitive Triangle is a simple but extremely effective technique to challenge inaccurate or unhelpful thinking, and it can be used in a variety of situations, including Justin's jealousy.

Couple: Misha and Sam

Prescription: Relationship Medicine: Playing Detective; Reflective Listening

Misha and Sam, like most couples, could benefit greatly from determining their primary attachment styles, just as Adam and Justin have done. They could also benefit from an exercise we call Playing Detective. By playing detective with our partners, we can find clues that tell us the meanings of their behaviors. *This doesn't mean that we're excusing bad behavior or allowing ourselves to be mistreated.* Rather, it means that we'll be able to better understand their actions so that we can problem-solve *together* how to prevent bad behavior or conflict in the future.

Playing Detective

When coaching couples, we encourage them to put their detective hats on when it comes to bad behavior. If we approach our partners' behaviors with the idea that every behavior has meaning, it allows us to take an observer position—which decreases the emotional intensity. Put on your best Sherlock Holmes hat and hold up a magnifying glass to your partner's (or your own) outrageous or hurtful behavior. Ask: "What might be the meaning of this behavior? What might be the feeling behind my partner's reaction? Is there anything from my partner's past that might explain this outlandish behavior?" In order to optimize your detective skills, you're going to have to learn how to create a space in your relationship to really understand your partner. That's where another tool—reflective listening—comes in!

Reflective Listening

This is a powerful tool we teach couples that can also be utilized with friends or family members or even in the workplace. And it's the same technique they teach us in How to Be a Therapist 101! The goal is not to solve the problem for the other person, but rather for the person on the receiving end to feel validated or understood. The internal feeling will be "he gets me" or "she really understands me." Once we're sure we're understood and our opinions are respected, we often are able to resolve issues before they turn from minor disagreements into major fights. Prior to initiating reflective listening, ensure that the two of you are not in the middle of a fight so that the body's alarm system doesn't hijack the conversation.

Reflective listening has ten steps:

1. Find a place to sit with your partner so that you're able to make eye contact with him or her. Using some sort of object (a cloth, a cup, whatever) to represent who has the speaking floor, begin the exercise with the person who possesses the object speaking; the other person doesn't get to talk until he or she is handed the object. During the discussion, you and your partner must hold hands and maintain eye contact to the extent that you can. The point is to get heart to heart. Note: This exercise is not intended to be conducted in the midst of a heated argument. Wait until things settle down before attempting this exercise, until the right mood is present, or things will not go well.

2. Introduce the conversation with "Help me understand . . ." or "I want to understand you." Let your partner know that you will listen until he or she is finished.

3. Allow your partner to speak freely without being interrupted. Focus intently on what your partner is saying to you, maintaining regular eye contact or nodding until your partner has finished what he or she is saying.

4. Check yourself during this conversation. Don't roll your eyes, sigh, or show strong reactions to what your partner is saying. Remember that you're trying to *understand the other person from his or her perspective*, not yours.

5. Paraphrase what your partner says: "What I hear you saying is . . ."

6. *Note your partner's feeling(s)* during this situation: "It sounds like that makes you feel . . ."

7. Fact check. Ask whether you understand correctly: "Do I have that right? Did I miss anything?"

8. Thank your partner for sharing with you, and let your partner know that you appreciate having a better understanding of his or her perspective.

9. *Apologize* for any way you contributed to the issue: "I'm sorry you felt that way—it was never my intention, but I realize that I hurt your feelings."

10. Tackle the problem. Now that your partner feels understood, the two of you can attack the problem together with the idea "It's not you versus me—it's *us versus this problem*."

So let's see how this process worked for Misha and Sam.

For example, Sam would approach Misha like this after Misha drank too much and picked a fight with him at a friend's party: He simply asked, "Help me understand what was going on with you last night." In doing so, Sam was searching for clues about what might be potential triggers for Misha. During these kinds of conversations, Misha talked about her difficult childhood and Sam learned more about her each time. Over time, she discussed a childhood in which she never really felt she was safe emotionally or that she was good enough. She always would be walking on eggshells at home and seeking approval from her mother and stability from her father. She told him about her father's chronic infidelity and how she was the one who would keep her mother from totally falling apart each time he cheated.

In one of these post-outburst conversations, Misha talked about how her father brought red roses home each time her parents reconciled. She would return home from school to see the flowers on the counter, and her heart would sink. In this conversation, it occurred to Sam that the previous evening, he'd given Misha a bouquet of—you guessed it—red roses before they left for the party. So, instead of feeling special or touched by this loving gesture by Sam, Misha felt annoyed and restless but could not quite figure out why. Suspecting some ulterior motive, her mind kept thinking, "Why is he giving me these roses?" Using reflective listening, Sam was able to hear Misha acknowledge feeling annoyed and restless, and he started to identify clues.

When they put the clues of the roses and acting out at the party together, the cause of her making a scene was understandable in a new context. This "aha" moment in their relationship was a game changer. Misha was able to see that she wasn't crazy but responded how one might expect her to based on what she went through earlier in her life. Sam was able to understand Misha's reaction and provide reassurance to her. They talked about some of Sam's triggers from his past too. His triggers stemmed from the unexpected death of his father when Sam was a young boy. He had his own baggage, such as fears of sudden loss, and his unusual, almost obsessive, focus on his health made a lot more sense to Misha once they worked through their baggage together. Using reflective listening, Misha was able to hear from Sam how he felt frustrated and helpless and sometimes overwhelmed and worried about her lack of trust in him and her subsequent behavior, which motivated her to work toward change.

As Sam continued to be steadfast, Misha's "tests" started to decrease over time. She would be surprised when he followed through on plans, really listened when she talked, and told her she was beautiful on the days when she felt her worst. Sam's emotional maturity allowed him to not be a doormat for Misha. Instead, he was what we call an "emotional container" for her.

How did he do this?

Sam set boundaries with Misha. When she was sneaking into his computer to check his work email, he sat her down and said, "I understand that a lot of men have betrayed you. I'm not them. I feel hurt when you accuse me of being interested in other women. I'm not interested in anyone but you. You will have to believe me because I will not allow you access to my email, and you're going to have to be OK with that." He provided a boundary, but he also provided loving reassurance that he was not going to betray her trust.

Of course, that one conversation didn't change everything. Consistency and reliability grew the trust between them and gave Misha the space to heal some of her past hurts because she could finally see that she had a soft and dependable place to land. Although it was hard for her not to engage in her typical dating-and-mating behaviors (e.g., checking to make sure he was cheating), eventually she was able to relax into the relationship, and their love grew stronger. Misha's anxiety lessened, her self-esteem dramatically improved, and she was flourishing at work and in life. Misha didn't "find herself" in her therapist's office, her trainer's gym, or her Zen garden. *She found herself within the context of a healthy relationship with Sam.*

How did that happen over time? Let's lay it out.

- Sam was empathic regarding Misha, which helped her to feel more comfortable.
- Misha let down her walls little by little to reveal pieces of her past to Sam even though it was not an easy thing for her to do. Using the Reflective Listening Medicine allowed her a vehicle to do this slowly.
- When Misha acted up, Sam would set a boundary in the moment. He would tell her he cared about her but that what she was doing was not OK. He set a time to talk when things were calmer either later that day or the next day, and they used reflective-listening skills to start to identify clues and triggers for Misha, as well as explore the feelings they each had related to their relationship.
- Most important, rather than getting furious at Misha's sometimes outrageous behaviors, Sam got curious and *put his detective hat on.*

Couple: Duke and Dana

Prescription: Relationship CPR: Individual and Couples Therapy; CPR Ground Rules

Arguably, Duke and Dana's marriage *should* have ended a long time ago. Although it is possible for many couples to move past infidelity and have an even stronger bond, getting over an affair—or multiple affairs—takes a lot of work from both partners. For those who are serial cheaters, the prospects of getting past this issue are gloomier. Both of us agree, however, that before a couple considers divorce and the painful experience that it likely entails, they want to be able to say, "We did everything we could to try to save our marriage." We also believe that people, with the right intervention, can change and recovery is possible. So, we offered some CPR suggestions for Duke and Dana.

Duke and Dana, hanging on to their marriage by a thread, each agreed to seek individual therapy. In therapy, Dana began exploring messages about marriage that she received growing up. She also processed living in a home where both parents were occasionally violent toward the other, creating an environment of instability and unpredictability. She discussed the pain of rejection from her husband, particularly after she became pregnant, and the pain of betrayal from his multiple affairs. Dana acknowledged that she stopped loving Duke at some point, once she realized she could not trust him to be faithful or have her best interests in mind, and loved only the idea of having married parents for her children. In the context of her own individual therapy, she discovered that her lack of consistency and predictability in her own upbringing actually led her to a series of relationships, including her marriage, that were mired in chaos and unpredictability—*because that was what was comfortable to her; it felt like home.*

Duke began working with an individual therapist, and as treatment progressed, it became clear that he needed to do more focused work on addiction, which he began, and he joined a support group for those struggling with sex or online addictions. In treatment, he was able to better understand why he sought out occasional one-night stands and why he became fascinated with women in online chat rooms—it went back to a deep-rooted fear of true intimacy and shame he had associated with experiences as a child and teenager in which people betrayed his trust or exploited him in some way, including inappropriate sexual activity with an older female babysitter. He also talked about how the emotional intimacy his wife seemed to have with her ex was intensely painful for him—and that this breach of trust to him seemed far worse than his one-night stands with women who meant nothing to him.

Simultaneously, Duke and Dana began couples work, and they decided that they would give it twelve months with both their couples therapy and individual work before making the decision to call it quits. Some CPR ground rules were enacted, such as cutting off communication with all extramarital interests—with wording that could be developed together and shared with the other partner. Duke and Dana created language like this: "I am focusing on repairing my marriage. As such, I can't continue to have any form of communication with you." Another CPR ground rule was both of them being open books to the other—meaning that they each had full access to the other's phone, computer, and other personal items. This rule sounds extreme (and contrary to the advice we may have given Misha and Sam), but in instances of severe breaches of trust, sometimes the only way to begin to come back from that is full transparency with the other person. At the time of writing this book, Duke and Dana are still together but continue to work with a couples therapist to facilitate communication between them. This was no easy feat. They did an enormous amount of work, individually and together, but they had the shared goals of repairing their marriage, restoring trust, and creating a new version of themselves—separately and together.

Summary

All three of these couples struggled with issues related to trust, and the baggage from their pasts was interfering with their ability to trust their partners in the present, to varying degrees. Everyone will have their own baggage that they bring into a relationship from their past, just like our couples did. For some, the baggage is pretty clear, but there will be other situations in which the suitcases are a lot more difficult to detect or are even invisible. That does not mean the suitcases—the baggage—don't exist. Armed with the right tools and techniques, such as understanding our partners' attachment styles, using reflective listening, and putting our detective hats on, we can better unpack what's going on and understand our partners so that we can prevent future relationship strain or arguments and ultimately strengthen our connections.

3

LACK OF
EMOTIONAL INTIMACY

I just don't feel connected to him. She doesn't understand me. He just doesn't get me. Talking to him is like talking to a wall. Why does she always freak out when I don't text back right away? Why do I feel so lonely even though we're always together?

What do all these statements have in common? These are reflections of people struggling to connect or struggling to safely connect emotionally to their partners. A lack of *emotional intimacy* can look like feeling misunderstood or unsupported by our partners, lonely, distant, or disconnected or having an overall lack of attention or concern from our partners. When couples are struggling or relationships fizzle out, it is often due to a lack of true emotional connection to each other. Although problems may first show up in their sex lives (see chapter 4 on sexual intimacy for tips on managing that), when issues between the sheets are a symptom that the relationship is struggling, sex usually isn't the origin of the problem. Relationships are not sustainable based purely on physical chemistry. Rather, it's a lack of true emotional connection—the connection that is built on emotional trust, vulnerability, emotional closeness, and acceptance—that's to blame.

The science is clear: We need strong emotional bonds to one another in order to thrive in this world. Emotional intimacy—having a strong base—affords us the security to feel more comfortable exploring the world. True emotional connection to partners allows us to be completely ourselves, flaws and all. If emotional intimacy is lacking and couples do not feel support, psychological safety, or overall connection, physical intimacy will suffer. Emotional intimacy is the foundation of a long-lasting relationship; therefore, it's critical that we invest what we can into nurturing those emotional connections with partners.

What's the recipe for solid emotional connection? We propose five ingredients: trust (as we discussed in chapter 2), intentional vulnerability, emotional expression, unwavering support, and special routines and rituals.

Vulnerability leads to increased trust and a stronger connection, as long as this vulnerability is intentional—meaning we're not saying to go throw yourself in a lion's cage and ask your partner to come and save you. Vulnerability means showing your partner the cracks in your exterior, the things you aren't proud of, the aspects about yourself that you perceive in some way as flawed.

It is hard to achieve emotional intimacy without talking about emotions themselves—that is, talking about your feelings! You didn't think you'd get away with reading this book with a psychologist and a sociologist not having you talk about feelings, did you? Couples who are able to increase their feelings vocabulary and communicate a wide variety of feelings to their partners using effective communication strategies are less likely to engage in maladaptive behaviors (such as scoffing, eye-rolling, and sarcasm) and are more likely to strengthen their emotional connections with one another.

A key ingredient to strengthening emotional connection is providing unwavering support. In order to achieve that strong emotional connection, we need our partners to know that we are their biggest cheerleaders—at work, at home, and in life. How do we do this? By showing up and providing what we call "predictable, compassionate availability," allowing our partners to be dependent on us when they want to, checking in with each other throughout the day, and providing comfort during difficult times. Allowing our partners to depend on us when they need to doesn't mean we're enabling them or micromanaging them—sometimes that support behind the scenes is just what they need to feel empowered. Additionally, we need to make sure we're using our words to cheer on our partners—daily compliments, praise, and appreciation can go a long way.

Part of emotional intimacy involves ensuring that both partners feel safe to communicate how they are feeling in different situations. Talking about feelings is easy for some but isn't always so easy for others. If you grew up in a home where the only feeling expressed was anger, talking about feeling embarrassed or insecure probably isn't in your wheelhouse.

The reason we do this is because not communicating directly about how we feel can lead to miscommunication and prevent us from having higher degrees of intimacy. We may be more comfortable expressing certain feelings like anger than we are expressing feeling embarrassed or ashamed, and we can sometimes forget to express our positive feelings about our partners too, leaving them feeling taken for granted.

The final, and often the most fun, ingredient is establishing special routines and rituals, plus making a commitment to planned spontaneity. Special routines and rituals are activities that you consistently do together, just the two of you. This could be something as simple as bringing your morning coffee to each other, always kissing before you separate, or taking a daily walk together after dinner. Planned spontaneity, by contrast, means that the two of you have committed to being spontaneous (even if you have to pick a day when you'll do it) when you do something new or different from what you've done before—something outside your Netflix and usual bar-and-grill date night. This approach can help stave off the relationship rut so many couples complain about and re-create the feelings you had in the earlier stages of your relationship.

We don't mean to sound like achieving a high degree of emotional intimacy is easy. It requires trust, vulnerability, and time—all of which require that we give something significant of ourselves. This is also a primary arena in which our past can affect our present, so our past experiences can make us avoid true emotional connection. Certain mental health difficulties (e.g., depression) can also make it more difficult to achieve emotional intimacy—and there are times when professional support is essential to help us achieve closeness in our relationships. However, with the right tools and support, we all can strengthen and nurture the emotional connections in our lives.

Let's take a look at three couples, all struggling with various issues related to emotional intimacy.

Couple #1: Britney and Marco: Mild Relationship Symptoms Related to Emotional Intimacy

Britney and Marco have been together for four years. Their physical chemistry was off the charts and they fell madly in love within weeks of meeting. Lately, however, Britney feels like she'd rather confide in her mother or girlfriends than Marco—and everything he does annoys her. Marco has been spending more time at the gym or fishing and has been saying, "I just need a break." Recently, Britney's sister moved in with them, and while Britney has enjoyed having her sister close, it has caused a strain on Britney and Marco's relationship.

Couple #2: Vadim and Sasha: Moderate Relationship Symptoms Related to Emotional Intimacy

Vadim and Sasha, together for twelve years, have hit a major rut in their marriage. They both work very hard at work and at home caring for their eight-year-old twin boys and five-year-old daughter. Their communication consists of short texts or conversations about what to make for dinner or pick up at the store, what the children's sports or activities schedules are, and an occasional (and obligatory) "How was your day?" Both of them say that despite being in the same home, they feel disconnected from each other— and, often, they communicate their frustrations with eye rolls, sarcasm (e.g., "Wow, you finally cleaned the kitchen; hell must have frozen over"), or mean barbs (e.g., "Well, you would feel better if you lost some weight; I'd lose weight if we actually had healthy meals instead of takeout every night").

Couple #3: Anu and Akmani: Severe Relationship Symptoms Related to Emotional Intimacy

Anu and Akmani have been together for six years. They have one child together. Although Anu would like to have more children, Akmani says that she is not sure this marriage is going to last and already feels as if she's raising their daughter on her own. Anu has a number of social groups he belongs to, many of which consist predominantly of women, while Akmani has said that she has to prioritize their child and does not have many outside interests. Anu, a passionate man, raises his voice when he is angry—but, in his defense, he raises his voice when he is also happy and excited. When Anu is upset about something, Akmani shuts down and retreats to her bedroom or the basement, where she watches movies with their daughter or does sudoku puzzles on her phone. Anu wonders where his once equally passionate wife has gone; Akmani has been fantasizing about life on her own with just her daughter and wonders whether Anu will just run off with one of those women from his groups.

All three of these couples are struggling with emotional connection. Look, it's inevitable that in most romantic relationships, the intensity of the passion dissipates to some degree. But in successful, happy relationships, that passionate love turns more toward compassionate love in which we have stable, loving foundations with partners who "get us." Couples who have been together for ten to thirty years and say they are still madly in love most often are not lying. Just because the initial intensity wanes doesn't mean you can't be madly in love with your partner decades later. In fact, brain research has suggested that in couples who have been married over twenty years, MRI scans reveal the same intensity of activity in dopamine-rich areas of the brain as couples who are newly in love, suggesting that the excitement of romance can remain while the nervousness that often comes with new love is what is lost. MRI scans show that the pattern of activity in the participants' dopamine reward systems is the same as that detected in the brains of participants in early-stage romantic love.[1] For those whose long-term marriages have transitioned from passionate, romantic love to a more compassionate, routine type of love, studies have shown that it's possible to rekindle the original flame. There are techniques and activities (including sexual activity; see chapter 4!) that can increase oxytocin levels and activate the brain's reward circuitry, which increases desire and emotional connection.

Our couples, however, are struggling to achieve even compassionate love with each other. Without the secure base of strong emotional connections with their partners, they have begun to avoid communication or find themselves drawn to other outlets or other people. Over time, this inattention to developing or nurturing their closeness has eroded the foundations of their relationships. Even though they are at different stages of severity, in each of these instances, the couples seem to be lacking richness in their relationships, and both partners feel as if their partners don't understand them and they would rather spend time with others or even be on their own.

In order to strengthen emotional intimacy, it can be helpful to have an understanding of our partners' primary attachment styles (see chapter 2). Those with a secure attachment style tend to struggle the least with achieving solid emotional intimacy in relationships—they trust easily, are more willing to be who they really are in relationships, and are able to look past perceived imperfections in others. Individuals with anxious attachment styles have difficulty establishing emotional intimacy due to a fear of being vulnerable with their partners (e.g., "If she knew how I really am, she'd leave me or love me less," or "If he knew about my past, he'd never look at me the same"). Individuals with anxious attachment styles struggle with trust, a necessary component in achieving true emotional intimacy. They are able to show up for partners and demonstrate consistent care and love for their partners, but at the same time, they are fearful that their partners may leave them or betray them—and this insecurity can undermine the relationships and prevents true emotional intimacy. Individuals with avoidant attachment styles will struggle the most with emotional intimacy, as the hallmark trait of an avoidant attachment style is to avoid true emotional closeness. For that reason, individuals with avoidant attachment styles (and those who love them) will need to work the most in this arena. Emotional intimacy does not come naturally—in fact, it may elicit fear. Knowing your attachment style, and your partner's, can give you some good data to figure out how best to proceed in developing a plan that makes sense for your relationship.

Keep the five ingredients to achieving emotional intimacy in mind: trust, intentional vulnerability, emotional expression, unwavering support, and special routines and rituals. No couple is going to achieve 100 percent perfection in any of these areas—but you can get a sense of where you may be lacking and where you could intervene in your own relationship to increase that emotional connection. Let's take a closer look at our couples to see how this situation plays out.

Britney and Marco: Mild Relationship Symptoms Related to Emotional Intimacy

Britney and Marco, while not complaining that they are unhappy with their marriage, each have been hoping that things will get better when Britney's sister moves out and they have their home back. That hope, however, is misguided. Truth be told, issues between them started prior to Britney's sister moving in—that intense passion, as it often does, had softened a bit between them. Britney's father died three years into her and Marco's relationship, which took a considerable toll on Britney. Marco, whose mother died when he was twelve, tried to be there for her the best that he could but noticed a shift in Britney after her father's death, and he felt useless. She became more irritable with him, and he felt like no matter what he did, he couldn't make her happy. So he distracted himself by fishing with his friends (or even by himself) and going to the gym. Marco got along fine with Britney's sister, but he secretly was jealous about the amount of time Britney and her sister were spending together—even though he was avoiding his wife! Britney found herself being annoyed at Marco for leaving his coffee cup on the table or his beer glass in the middle of the living room, feeling like "I'm always cleaning up after him" and "he can spend all this time going fishing but can't take two seconds to clean up after himself." Her annoyance increased to rage, and one night she threw the coffee cup in the sink and broke it, screaming, "Why don't you pick up your own damn cup? When's the last time you picked up anything of mine?" Marco screamed back, "Maybe if you weren't too busy watching *Housewives* with your sister, you'd notice what I do for you around here!" It didn't take a rocket scientist (or even a psychologist) to figure out that this intensity was about much more than the coffee cup. In fact, both of them, although they did not have the vocabulary or the awareness (yet), wanted the same things—to reconnect to each other and to feel needed and understood by the other. After Britney's father died, her grief was all-consuming. She was from a close-knit family, and her father was one of her biggest champions. But for some reason, she could not talk about the rawness she felt with Marco—all she could do was cry. When her sister moved in, she felt a relief. When Britney's father died, Marco tried to be there for Britney by hugging her when she was crying, but at the same time, he said, "I just froze." He said that he, too, was initially relieved when Britney's sister moved in. "She seemed to comfort her in a way I just couldn't." But then the dynamic in the household significantly changed.

Vadim and Sasha: Moderate Relationship Symptoms Related to Emotional Intimacy

Vadim and Sasha have had many years of happiness together—but over the past five years, both have expressed concerns to each other and to trusted friends that they aren't happy. Neither of them wants to pursue a divorce, but they both want something more. The business of life—managing jobs, raising children (including children with special learning needs), and doing numerous activities—has had them communicating about what needs to get accomplished before the next thing, and they have been going off in different directions. Vadim, who is heavily into his children's sports and extracurricular activities, tries to balance this with his heavy workload as a veterinarian. Sasha, who is an accountant, manages the household finances and focuses her attention on making sure the children's educational and medical needs are met—she's in charge of all medical and dental appointments and is the "liaison" to their school, as they have two children who are on IEPs and require additional educational advocacy. Sasha, while she appreciates Vadim's investment in their extracurricular activities, says, "I feel like I never get to turn it off—I'm always worried about someone or something in this house." When asked about the spark between them, both of them joke, "What spark?" and they have acknowledged that when it comes to sex, they would rather sleep or watch television.

Sasha has expressed that she is unhappy in her job and believes that it may not actually be a career she wants to continue. She chose accounting because "numbers make sense" and she knew that she would make a solid income, but as she has worked more closely with her children's school, she has wondered whether she might prefer to work as an educational advocate or a special-education teacher. Vadim has minimized her desire for a change, saying, "Nobody's job is perfect." Vadim, once an avid tennis player, hasn't picked up a racket in over two years, saying that he doesn't have time for any extracurriculars for himself. Sasha rolls her eyes, saying, "All he liked about tennis was the drinks at the club afterward."

While one might argue that these two could simply be at a Vitamins level and that their problems and quibbles are mild, their shared dissatisfaction has gone on for years and, without intervention, likely will go on for many more—meaning that they could have *decades* of their lives together during which they are less than happy. If Vadim and Sasha can master a few basic techniques and make some adjustments to their family rhythms, it is possible that not only could they be happier, but their relationship would also be richer and more meaningful, and they could strengthen the home they have created for their children.

Anu and Akmani: Severe Relationship Symptoms Related to Emotional Intimacy

Anu and Akmani fell in love after a whirlwind courtship—Akmani loved Anu's fiery spirit; Anu loved Akmani's zest for life and unyielding optimism. Anu would joke that "Akmani could find the good in garbage," and he loved this quality. They were engaged six months after they met and married a year later. They enjoyed hiking and cooking and shared a love of the arts.

Akmani became pregnant, and their daughter, Anori, was born four years into their marriage. While they had some of the same complaints most new parents do (e.g., exhaustion, feeling overwhelmed, and not having enough "me" time), both of them thoroughly enjoyed being parents. Akmani, who had a difficult pregnancy and labor, had decreased her work hours during her pregnancy and worked part-time as a social media manager for a clothing brand, and she maintained this lighter work schedule so that she could care for Anori. At the same time, Anu was promoted in his role as a pharmaceutical rep for a major drug company. His work hours didn't change, but the number of social obligations (e.g., dinners and lunches) increased in order to attract new clients. He also continued to be actively involved in the groups that he and Akmani participated in in the past—an arts club, an outdoor-adventure social group, and a supper club for foodies. Due to a number of factors—pregnancy, the pandemic, and caring for a baby and toddler—Akmani no longer participated in these activities, nor did she join Anu for any of his work dinners. She remarked, "He's created his life—and from all appearances, it's a life without me." Anu likes being social and continuing to stay involved with all the activities they enjoyed while they were dating and married before their first child—"It's how we stay young!" he would exclaim to his wife—and he does not understand why she does not join him during his work events, even when he has told her that she is invited.

2

Anu has repeatedly told Akmani that he wants more children, about which Akmani says, "He can't have it all—does he want a wife or a mother to his children?" When she turned down his multiple invitations to join him or his suggestions that they get a babysitter, he got angry. And when Anu was angry, especially after returning from an outing with other couples, he would unleash this dissatisfaction on Akmani through loud exclamations about how she was missing out and would say, "What do you think people think about me when I show up time and time again with no wife?" He slammed doors and, more recently, called her names such as "heartless" and "boring," saying, "Everyone thinks you must be a cold bitch, and I'm starting to think they are right." Akmani, with tears in her eyes, said nothing and took her daughter to the basement to put on the latest Disney movie. Young Anori has recently been acting up, stomping around, slamming doors, and yelling at her mother. Akmani recently confided in her sister that there is no way she will have another child with Anu because "I'll just be raising two children on my own instead of one" and that she is thinking about a divorce. She said, "I hope he has an affair," just to give her a reason to go through with it.

RELATIONSHIP Rx FOR EACH COUPLE

Couple: Britney and Marco

Prescription: Relationship Vitamins: Vulnerability Exercise—Regrets and Struggles; Decide on a Daily Ritual

Vulnerability Exercise—Regrets and Struggles

Britney and Marco are struggling with a common phenomenon that happens in relationships—both are tiptoeing around the other and not bringing up conflict or hurt because they don't want to rock the boat. Britney and Marco were assigned a vulnerability exercise and instructed to each write down their responses to three questions:

1. What is your biggest regret or something you wish you could have done differently in your life?

2. What are you struggling with the most right now as an individual?
3. What are you struggling with the most right now as a couple?

Then they met together to share their responses, taking turns. After each completed sharing, the other partner asked, "What can I do to support you in this?" and "What do you need from me?"

Often, conflict happens in relationships just because we don't have all the data—meaning that we don't truly understand where the other is coming from or how to understand his or her behavior. In psychology, we have the term *mentalizing*, which means keeping the other person's mind in mind. When we keep their mind on our mind, we can increase secure attachment and connection—but in order to keep our partner's mind in mind, we need to ensure that we understand him or her. In our fast-paced, action-oriented world, it's easy to jump to conclusions or go straight into problem-solving mode, but doing so can leave our loved ones feeling that we don't care or don't really understand them. Reflective listening, which we discussed in chapter 2, is a great tool to help increase our understanding. Getting curious instead of furious about our partners' behavior—working to understand the meaning of their behavior—is another strategy. One way to get a better understanding of what our partners are struggling with is to engage in conversations about vulnerabilities, such as regrets.

Interestingly, both Britney and Marco said that when it came to their biggest regrets, they each wished that they had savored the time with their parents prior to their deaths. Britney said she wished she hadn't rushed her father off the phone or had made spending time with him a priority in recent years; Marco said that he wished he knew more about his mother and regretted that she was never able to meet Britney. When asked what they could do to support each other, Britney confessed that she did not feel comfortable talking with Marco because he lost his mother—although she knew he would understand, she felt guilty that she had so many years with her father and that Marco lost so much by not having his mother throughout his childhood. At the same time, she felt like Marco wasn't there for her in the way she needed him to be, and until her sister moved in, "I felt like I was grieving alone." Marco said that watching Britney and being at the funeral "brought it all back for me." He talked about what it was like as a child to have to bury his mom and how, when people talked to him, he "just froze and went numb." His father struggled with talking about his mother's death, "so we just didn't talk about it," and he said, "That's all I know to do." They both wanted to be there for each other, but they didn't know how—Britney because she didn't want to burden Marco but at the same time was resentful in not getting her needs met, and Marco because his childhood template of freezing and numbing and just not talking about it was activated when he saw Britney suffer.

In sharing their responses to the second question, the primary issue that Britney was struggling with was also grieving her father: "It's been a year. I just still feel so sad." Marco said that the primary issue he was struggling with was feeling lonelier than usual. When asked what they could do for the other, Marco said that he would love to spend more time just talking with Britney—even about her father—and said, "I miss him too." Britney said that she'd love to be able to talk with Marco when she was having a rough day, acknowledging that it was easier to talk with her sister because they had the shared loss.

When it came to the question about struggling in their relationship, Britney said that she felt disconnected from Marco. Marco said, "I just miss the two of us having fun together without all the heaviness of life." Both Britney and Marco said that what they needed from the other was shared time to talk but also to enjoy each other. According to Dr. John Gottman, expressing a *positive need* is a recipe for success for both the listener and the speaker because it conveys complaints and requests without criticism and blame.[2] Instead of thinking about what is wrong with our partners, if we transform our thinking to "what I feel and what I need from you," we can make major shifts in our relationships without anyone feeling defensive.

Decide on a Daily Ritual

Both Britney and Marco laughed about how Britney's sister moving in was a relief as well as a distraction. They said that they need to prioritize their own special time with each other and so agreed to schedule early-morning walks together and then a happy hour (even if it was just tea), just the two of them, on their deck in the evenings. Creating new routines and rituals together did a few things for Britney and Marco beyond meeting their expressed need to spend more time talking with one another. Predictability in the form of routines and rituals actually sends signals to the brain that we are safe. If we have bedtime rituals or goodbye rituals with our partners, that predictability can improve our own well-being and deepen our connections by signaling to our brains that we are safe.

Couple: Vadim and Sasha

Prescription: Relationship Medicine: What I Miss about Us; What's in Your Crayon Box?; "But Out"; "I Feel" Statements; Intentional Affirmations; Cheerleader Role Play

What I Miss about Us

Vadim and Sasha, having been together for a long time, have fallen into a common relationship rut in which they have taken each other for granted and resentment has grown over the years. Sasha feels like she does everything for their family and carries the largest cognitive and emotional load, compared to Vadim, who "just has to run [the kids] to their practices." Vadim feels like he never stops moving for their family and is completely taken for granted. They have forgotten why they became a couple in the first place and what made them want to spend their lives together. Like it or not, having children has a significant impact on marriage, which we will talk about in future chapters. What sometimes happens is that couples don't realize the impact until much later—often it's years before they ask, "What the hell happened to us?" A simple exercise Vadim and Sasha can start with is taking time to write to each other what they miss about their relationship, with each of them reflecting on their early years together, their favorite attributes about the other person, and what made them "work" in the first place. They can then share their letters with each other—by reading each letter aloud to the other person. This process will allow them to start difficult conversations on a positive note and conjure up feelings of connection and endearment.

What's in Your Crayon Box?

Both Vadim and Sasha struggle with expressing emotions other than annoyance and anger. Like many couples, they could benefit from increasing their feelings vocabularies and expressing their feelings more effectively using "I feel" statements and "but outs." They could also benefit from intentionally expressing positive affirmations to each other. When we think about increasing our feelings vocabularies, think about a crayon box—those tiny crayon boxes they give you at restaurants with a few colors. We want to get to a place where we feel more comfortable talking about the crayon box with eighty different colors. We have an activity couples can use to start practicing this skill. Start by thinking about a recent situation that caused some distress and go through a feelings vocabulary list to identify the feelings that resonated most with that event. For a downloadable list of over 270 feelings words that you can print and use free of charge, go to https://www.berkeleywellbeing .com/uploads/1/9/4/8/19481349/printable-list-of-emotions.pdf. Then, using reflective listening (outlined in chapter 2), practice talking with your partner, identifying a minimum of three feelings related to that event other than the primary feelings in the little crayon box—happy, sad, or angry.

"But Out"

Vadim and Sasha were also given strategies for effective communication about feelings related to conflict between them. First, they were advised to "but out," meaning to watch their language and replace every "but" with "and." Using the word "but" sets up a scenario in which our partners feel their concerns are dismissed and not considered—and immediately puts the other person on the defensive. For example, "I love you, *but* we need to look at how we spend money" feels different from "I love you, *and* we need to look at how we spend money." "We're spending the holidays at your family's house this year, *but* next year I want to spend time at mine" feels different from "We're spending the holidays at your family's house this year, *and* next year I want to spend time at mine." By changing one simple word in our communication, we have the opportunity to join with our partners instead of putting them on the defensive.

"I Feel" Statements

A straightforward communication technique for couples (and you can use this in other relationships too!) is to use "I feel" statements to express our concern or dissatisfaction with situations or conflicts, referencing that crayon box of feelings we talked about earlier.

For example, the impact is different when you say "You don't do anything around the house" from when you say "I feel stressed out and overwhelmed because I think I'm doing the lion's share of the work around the house."

Here are a couple more examples:

- "You don't let me say what I want to do when it comes to making plans" versus "I feel frustrated when we talk about making plans and I don't get to say what I want to do. I want us both to have input."
- "You're always going out and leaving me home alone" versus "I feel angry and left out when I am alone and you are out with your friends. I would like to be invited to be with you, even if you are with your friends."

Intentional Affirmations

Instead of focusing on venting their frustrations to each other, Vadim and Sasha were charged with intentionally expressing feelings to each other about three positive qualities or actions in their partner every day. Examples could include the following: "I feel loved when you bring my coffee to me in the morning." "I feel relieved when you do things like clean up after the kids' dinner, as it's one less thing for me to do." "I feel more confident about myself going into my day when you kiss me goodbye and give me one of those squeezy hugs."

Cheerleader Role Play

Similar to Britney and Marco, Vadim and Sasha likely will benefit from the strategy of expressing positive needs. Asked to channel their best cheerleaders (costumes not necessary), Vadim and Sasha were instructed to ask each other, "Where can I show up for you?" They challenged each other to think about the different areas of their life they were struggling with and to practice their "fancy with their feelings" strategies. Sasha said that she would like for Vadim to help her more with managing some of the day to day and to help her brainstorm how they could work together to ensure that she wasn't always in the role of the "house manager." She asked Vadim to join her at the children's IEP meetings when possible and said that she would try to schedule them during a time that worked with his schedule so that he could be there. She then added that although he wasn't keen on her looking into different career options, she wanted his support—even if she just explored what those options might look like. Vadim said that he felt stressed and pressured, as he was worried what would happen if his wife stopped working to pursue her education and leave the solid job that she had. She agreed that she would not leave her current job until she had a plan in place for how she might pursue additional educational experience while not putting additional burdens on their family. Vadim talked about how he missed tennis and part of that was the social connection he felt—like "I have a space in the world outside of the vet clinic and home." He also acknowledged that he wanted to get back into better shape, so he would love for Sasha to work with him to brainstorm how he could join a tennis league and still be present for her and their family. They found a league close to their home that played on Tuesdays and Saturday mornings. Sasha agreed to take the kids to more of their sports practices, which she realized she actually enjoyed because she got to turn her brain off while they were on the field.

Both Vadim and Sasha felt better supported by the other, and each reported that they had a much higher degree of feeling understood by the other. Although they first joked about how it was hard to come up with three positive statements about the other, they came to find that they enjoyed doing this—and it was a good reminder of all that they loved about each other. Although it wasn't necessarily the intention, they said their sex life had never been better (the connection between emotional intimacy and sexual intimacy is one we will get into in the next chapter!).

Couple: Anu and Akmani

Prescription: Relationship CPR: What I Miss about Us; Couples Therapy

Anu and Akmani are in serious relationship trouble, and now their young child, Anori, has begun to act out the conflict between them. Akmani has withdrawn out of a fear response to Anu and has resorted to retreating to the bedroom or basement to avoid his anger. Anu no longer feels supported by his wife—he feels rejected and embarrassed that she no longer wants to spend time with him. However, we don't think this is a couple who should be calling a divorce attorney just yet. Professional intervention can uncover their poor communication and help them develop strategies to return to a place in their relationship where they both feel emotionally safe and supported.

In therapy, Anu and Akmani were given some relationship ground rules, given the intensity of things at home—no name-calling whatsoever, no slamming of doors, and calling a relationship time-out (e.g., take at least a twenty-minute break from each other by doing a task such as reading a magazine, gardening, etc.) and then a time-in (agreeing to come back together after a certain amount of time—"let's talk in an hour") when there was a conflict. They developed a code word—"chipmunk"—for when Akmani felt triggered by Anu's raised voice, with the ground rule that Anu must lower his voice immediately or take a twenty-minute break before revisiting the conversation if he was feeling too upset. The couples therapist was very clear that if they could not abide by these ground rules (e.g., Akmani didn't feel safe enough to use the code word or Anu continued to call her names or yell), they needed to meet with individual therapists to work on these separate issues.

In meeting with Akmani and Anu, the couples therapist asked about the relationships they observed in their own childhoods. It was during this conversation that Akmani opened up about having a father who struggled with his mental health and would berate her mother—and, at times, physically hurt her. Akmani said that she never wanted a relationship like that—and although Anu had not physically harmed her, his emotionally abusive language was unacceptable. The therapist explained that it would be difficult for Akmani to be able to feel emotionally safe or connected when voices were raised—that it was likely she was triggered in some way and she did what she knew to protect herself, which was retreat from Anu and take her daughter with her. Akmani used "I feel" statements in therapy to communicate how she felt, saying, "I feel tense and nervous when you raise your voice. . . . Sometimes I just go numb, but I feel like I have to escape." Anu explained that he had always been a yeller, even when he was excited about something, and that "if I don't yell, I feel like you don't listen to me or take me seriously." The therapist explained that by yelling, he actually wasn't getting her attention—in fact, he was getting the opposite of what he actually wanted. Thus the ground rules were even more important for this relationship to work. Anu, although he knew a little about Akmani's childhood, did not know the specifics. Ashamed of how he made his wife feel, he was motivated to change his communication style and pay more attention to his tone and the messaging.

After they agreed to these ground rules, Anu and Akmani were given the same exercise that Vadim and Sasha completed, What I Miss about Us, and instructed to write their letters but wait until the next session to read them aloud to each other. Anu read his letter to Akmani, noting that he missed "the way you used to look at me" and how she would always lift his spirits, even when he was down on himself. He missed their shared interests—their love for food and culture. He also wrote about how he missed when they would attend events together—"Just having you there made me feel like a better man"—and that he yearned for her company, even when he was surrounded by other people. Changing his "but" to an "and" (with the guidance of their therapist), he said, "I love our daughter deeply *and* I also miss my wife." Akmani read her letter to Anu, saying that she missed feeling emotionally connected and "even though we're different, you get me." She said that she also missed feeling carefree in their relationship and missed "that feeling where I wake up happy to be together." She acknowledged that she had always loved his passion but missed being able to appreciate this quality in him, as her appreciation seemed to be overshadowed by building resentment. She wrote, "I miss having a partner" and "I miss feeling understood and accepted." Akmani also wrote, "I know motherhood has shuffled my priorities," and she, too, missed "how we used to try different foods together—dining out or cooking in" and discovering new local artists together. As is true with many couples, they both actually wanted the same thing, for their partner to be accepting and consistently available for them—to show up for them—but they had no idea how to get there. With the guidance of the couples therapist, they agreed that Anu would prioritize some (but not all) of his work or social outings that he really wanted his wife to attend with him, and twice per month they would each choose an activity that did not have any work obligations (e.g., getting to know a local artist, visiting a new restaurant) that they would try. Akmani would find a sitter or a family member whom she was comfortable with to watch Anori. They agreed that they would try this new plan for a few months and reevaluate the relationship at that point. Akmani agreed that if they worked on "us for a year," then she would put having another child back on the table.

Summary

All three couples struggled with various issues related to emotional intimacy. Emotional intimacy means emotional closeness. That closeness involves trust and creating relationships that are consistent, reliable (so we can learn to depend on one another), and compassionate—in which we are free to be who we truly are and are accepted for our flaws. By paying attention to five main areas—trust (as we discussed in chapter 2), intentional vulnerability, emotional expression, unwavering support, and special routines and rituals—and making modifications to those areas we think may be falling short, couples can significantly increase their emotional intimacy. Having that solid emotional connection makes for more satisfying relationships and more resilient couples—who are better able to handle all that life will throw at them, together.

4

LOSS OF SEXUAL INTIMACY AND ATTRACTION

We used to have sex all the time, but now we never do! Is my partner even attracted to me anymore? We aren't as physically connected as I want to be—we barely even cuddle. Our sex life isn't what it used to be. He thinks about me as only his sexual outlet—not a person! I'm too tired for sex! We had a baby and now I can't think of myself as a sexual being, only a parent.

What differentiates a close friendship from a lover or spouse? Not a tough question. It is primarily sexual attraction and sexual intimacy. And in more cases than not, it is that initial spark of sexual interest that moves two people closer, eager to find out whether there is more there than just physical attraction.

That attraction is something of a mystery—or at least we don't fully understand why it's so strong from even the slightest observation of that person. Whether you believe that attraction is simply from pheromones (we don't) or because this person is your ideal physical template or because the person reminds you of your first crush, you recognize the signs: You gaze into each other's eyes more intently than you ever would do with just a friend, you have butterflies in your stomach, or your entire body feels like it's on red alert. And we know you know what we're talking about!

This physical attraction can be so strong or so intense that sometimes it is mistaken for love or (if not love) the reason for pursuing the promise of love with this person. If the attraction hangs around for a while—maybe even a long time—it becomes the basis for trying to make this relationship work. It is, as some people have described it, a drug, and we hear statements like "I am addicted to him" and even "I know I should leave, but I can't get enough of her." Desire is a powerful feeling and is perhaps, as the noted biological anthropologist Helen Fisher describes it, a drive that is every bit as primal as our drive for food or even survival. Couple that with love—also wired into our brains' internal drive systems, according to Fisher—and that wiring explains a lot besides pleasure and deep feelings of connectedness; it can also explain some of the foolish and desperate acts we do during dating, mating, and marriage.[1]

Despite not fully understanding how the attraction occurs initially, the science is clear: We need human contact, especially in the form of physical contact. In a sense, touch is medicine. A long embrace releases oxytocin, the hormone in our bodies often referred to as the "love drug" that helps create an emotional connection to another person, improves our mood, calms our nervous systems, lowers our blood pressure, and improves our immune functioning. Touching and being touched (when wanted) activates certain areas of our brains and causes the release of dopamine and serotonin, other feel-good hormones in our brains that can help reduce anxiety and depression, while at the same time reducing stress hormones like cortisol and norepinephrine. Sexual intimacy can do the same thing—to an even greater degree.

So it is not surprising that when our attraction wanes or our sex lives are challenged or are in jeopardy, it is likely to lead to some sort of relationship train wreck. In fact, even minor dissatisfactions in the bedroom can erode a relationship that has a lot of things going for it (e.g., "We're really great roommates" or "He's great with the kids"). But those other things going for them may not be enough to keep a couple together—or, if together, keep them happy.

Let's look at three couples in varying levels of distress.

Couple #1: Benito and Ariana: Mild Relationship Symptoms Related to Sex and Attraction

Our first couple, Benito and Ariana, is a young couple whose sex life has been disrupted by the distractions of work and a new baby, as well as some body-image concerns.

Couple #2: Karlee and Anderson: Moderate Relationship Symptoms Related to Sex and Attraction

Our second couple, Karlee and Anderson, feel unattracted to each other and now rarely have sex because they have become constantly argumentative. A deep and abiding anger over repeated conflicts that never get resolved has resulted in them sleeping in separate bedrooms, and when they do have sex, it feels robotic and unsatisfactory for both of them.

Couple #3: Glenn and Bernard: Severe Relationship Symptoms Related to Sex and Attraction

Our third couple, Glenn and Bernard, are at odds over one spouse's individual decision that monogamy isn't important to him and that his partner needs to adjust to his change of heart. Secretly, Glenn has also been taking his sexual desire for live-sex pornographic images to the extreme and is spending extended hours in his office watching live sex online, a fact that his partner has only recently discovered.

Even though our couples are at very different places in their intimate and sexual lives, they all want essentially the same things—to be desired and to physically connect with each other. It is not unusual for couples to argue about their sex lives or have differing opinions about the frequency of what they think is acceptable in their relationship. In fact, most couples will have disagreements about sex from time to time. We have found that when couples are struggling in other realms of their relationships (see the preceding chapters on trust and emotional intimacy), their satisfaction in the bedroom is a good barometer for their overall relationship satisfaction. Couples who aren't sexually satisfied are more likely to have problems in other arenas too. Our three couples' waning sex lives and conflicts over sex are hindering one of the ways they could actually offset the stress in their lives and improve their overall well-being—inside and outside the bedroom. Instead of addressing their lack of physical connection, they have allowed it—and the lack of communication about it—to create wedges between them.

Let's take a closer look at all three couples and the conflicts they are having related to their sex lives.

Benito and Ariana: Mild Relationship Symptoms Related to Sex and Attraction

Benito and Ariana are in their mid-twenties and have been married two years but together four years. Before they were married, their sex life was hot and heavy, but now, with a ten-month-old baby and long work hours, they rarely have sex and Benito is unsatisfied and angry about it. He says that he doesn't vent his feelings out loud, "but I am angry and frustrated and feel like there is a bait and switch going on. . . . I mean, when we were dating, we were all over each other. Now, it's like nothing. . . . But I don't tell her this in an angry tone because then she will just shut down and we don't talk for days." At the same time, Ariana feels unappreciated and hassled by her husband. She says that she is almost constantly in a bad mood, and when it comes to sex, she just "doesn't feel it." What she does feel is fat (she has twenty extra pounds from weight she gained during her pregnancy and from being stuck in the house during the COVID-19 shutdowns) and unattractive (she feels her body is no longer toned and pretty), and she believes Benito's "demands" are unreasonable. She tells Benito that she is sure once she loses weight and the baby is older, things will get better. Ariana says, "Benito just has to wait. . . . Is that too much to ask? You know, having a baby is a big deal, and I think Benito doesn't understand that it comes with changes, and I'm tired *all the time* and he just doesn't get it."

Meanwhile, they haven't had sex in more than five months, and Benito, who started out being supportive and understanding, has now lost patience. He says he is not the kind of man who cheats, but he does find himself looking at other women and fantasizing about having sex with them. He says, "I feel this is dishonorable," and he also feels it is dishonorable not to confess these fantasies to his wife and be honest with her. So he did, which unfortunately hurt her deeply and has made her feel even worse about herself, as well as angry and even less inclined to take her clothes off in front of him, much less have sex. Ariana also expresses her concern that although he has not voiced this feeling out loud to her, Benito isn't interested in her or pleasing her; he just wants to "get his" and move on, saying, "I feel like I'm either a mom or a piece of meat to him. . . . There's no in between."

While all too common, particularly after the transition to parenthood, this can be a tough situation. However, we feel it can be reversed with some basic tools and strategies at the Vitamins level of care, which we will detail below. But our second couple, Karlee and Anderson, are in a more complex and hard-to-reverse situation.

Karlee and Anderson: Moderate Relationship Symptoms Related to Sex and Attraction

Karlee and Anderson have been together for seven years. They are in their mid-thirties, and they are constantly fighting about a number of issues, including whether to have a child and whether to move into a different home. During these fights, it is not uncommon for one of them (usually Karlee) to go into the guest bedroom and end up sleeping there for several nights. While sex was never the focal point of their relationship, it now happens rarely, and both say that it feels mechanical and unrewarding. Karlee remarks, "Never mind sex! He doesn't even touch me. It used to be a day or two, but now we can go a week without him so much as touching my back or holding my hand."

But it's not just sex that is stalled and problematic; Karlee and Anderson have stopped spending quality, focused time together. When they were younger, there was always a sacred date night. As work increased and their tempers flared more often, they stopped getting dressed up and going out together. They stopped double-dating with friends. Over time, they fell into a routine in which they would turn on Netflix and binge-watch shows at night when they got into bed together—and while doing so allowed them to turn off their brains from their day, it eroded the time they could have had for connection. They also talk less than they used to. Both say that it doesn't feel safe to communicate with each other because it will break out into a fight and they are trying to keep the peace. Karlee says, "He always thinks I'm out to get him," while Anderson believes, "I swear she doesn't hear what I am saying to her. I think I am just talking to myself half the time." They both feel undesired, unwanted, and constantly judged by the other. They long for more connection with each other, but both have said, "I don't know how we got here," and they don't know how to stop this cycle they are in.

Glenn and Bernard: Severe Relationship Symptoms Related to Sex and Attraction

Glenn and Bernard, ages fifty and sixty-two, respectively, have been together for over twenty years but are at the point of breaking up. They had an agreement, renewed at their recommitment ceremony ten years ago, that they would be monogamous, but Glenn has broken that trust several times and lately has leaned into his belief that monogamy does not make sense. Moreover, Glenn spends hours in his office many nights per week, which Bernard thought was an addiction to work but now has discovered is an addiction to porn. Glenn feels that because Bernard is a gay man, Bernard is making too big a deal over Glenn's sexual habits, but in turn Glenn has offered Bernard the option of also seeking sex outside the relationship. However, that is not how Bernard wants their relationship to operate, and he is deeply hurt by Glenn's insistence on non-monogamy and the new revelation that Glenn has been spending hours on live-sex pornography sites online. He thought Glenn was on the same page that he was, but now he sees that Glenn has been living a parallel life, both with other men and with pornography. Bernard, who had always imagined that he and Glenn would grow old together, is now seeing their twenty-three-year union in immediate danger of dissolving. Glenn sees it as well, but he is in the midst of his latest infatuation with a much younger man. He says, "Bernard is simply too possessive and too insecure. He's seen me with young men before, and he knows it will burn itself out. I don't think he will really leave, although he's always threatening to."

RELATIONSHIP Rx FOR EACH COUPLE

Couple: Benito and Ariana

Prescription: Relationship Vitamins: Work Out to Work It Out; Schedule the Sex

Our first couple was in a pretty typical situation for new parents, but it didn't give Benito comfort that he had friends going through the same problem. But it does help if we think of something as a phase rather than as a future. New mothers and fathers in the first years of child-raising are famously fatigued and spread thin, and they often range from being simply extra grouchy to having more significant (but very common) diagnoses of postpartum depression or postpartum anxiety. In her premarital and early-marriage coaching sessions, Dr. Jessica advises couples who are planning families to change their mindsets that parenting changes one's life to "parenthood doesn't change your life, but it *ends the life you formerly had.*" You have a new life now—it is richer than the prior one, but that does not mean there is not also loss of that former life. This view sounds extreme, but if couples are better prepared for the dramatic shift, tension and resentments can be avoided or at least minimized. (See chapter 11 for more on children and parenting.) Spontaneity, who is in control of your day, what constitutes a good night's sleep, and even having fun look different after you have a child. Both partners can yearn for the sexual intimacy they had prior to having children, but often work and time with the baby put sex on the back burner and contribute to couples feeling frustrated, resentful, or disconnected. This situation is *extremely common* with new parents, and we cannot emphasize that enough—which is why it is critically important to identify this as an issue and have tools and strategies to help you when you're too tired and the baby (and, for many, more babies) takes priority. Sleep deprivation is one of the major causes of sexual disinterest (for both parents) and is not to be underestimated. When we're not sleeping, we're dysregulated emotionally and physically, so we are less likely to be physically aroused in the way we are if we're rested. In addition to lack of sleep, the constant emotional and physical care that children require coupled with work-related and other stressors can deplete our energy so that a shower, Netflix, or a nap sounds so much more exhilarating than getting ready to go out on a date together.

Still, even though this is a potentially serious situation that needs rectifying before months turn into years, it doesn't need to have a super-complex answer. What it does need is recognition by both partners that this situation isn't good for the marriage and has to be addressed, along with commitment to set a plan or a schedule of reconnection that they take seriously. Couples can address how this is not good for their marriages through having clear communication and practicing reflective listening sessions (reviewed in chapter 2). We offer some additional Vitamins prescriptions related to developing a plan that will be both doable and effective.

Work Out to Work It Out

One way to break this stalemate or endless cycle of "we haven't had sex, we feel disconnected and resentful, so we don't want to have sex, and we get more resentful" is to make a plan to do something about it. A simple strategy that couples can use that will have plentiful benefits is prioritizing physical exercise and developing a routine that also includes finishing the workout, eating a healthy meal together, and determining when "sexy time" will happen. Exercise really is the magic ingredient for health, improved mood, more regulated sleep, and feelings of sexual attractiveness. While Ariana may not suddenly have lost all the weight she had gained, she would definitely feel better with an improved mood. (Research has shown that exercise can reduce symptoms of depression by up to 40 percent—equal to most antidepressants![2]) When she was feeling better emotionally, and when she felt stronger and more toned, that would do wonders for regaining sexual desire. In addition to improved blood flow throughout the body, another benefit is that the chemicals released during exercise increase physiological arousal in both men and women and combat the dreaded stress chemical cortisol, which is a mood and libido slayer. It may have taken a while to figure out a pattern that worked, but this couple could work out together three (or more) times per week, even if it was for just thirty minutes. (If there was no babysitter, they could find a gym that had childcare on-site or ask a trusted family member to assist with the baby.) They could finish with a light lunch or dinner (depending on what time of day worked best for them). As soon as the baby was asleep, they could grab the time and set aside the afternoon or evening for sexual play or physical connection (even a post-workout massage they offered one another could help with that connection), and they could start re-creating their sexual spark. Ariana and Benito could also work together to set up a plan to help each of them maximize his or her sleep, which was already guaranteed to improve if a regular exercise regimen was put in place. Getting into a regular exercise routine is advice other therapists may have given them, but, honestly, following this advice—simply getting more fit and creating space while one is in a good mood for sexual intimacy—will rather quickly move couples from sexless marriages to better sexual connections. That is, as long as it actually is body image, sleep deprivation, and the transition from "we into three" that are the issues, as opposed to more deep-seated anger, disrespect, contempt (see chapter 7), or other serious problems.

Schedule the Sex

The second strategy we suggest to couples who are not on the same page when it comes to their preferences for frequency of sex, or to couples who just want to make their sex lives a priority, is to schedule the sex. Dr. Jessica has a colleague who has been married for forty years, and he has told her the secret to his and his partner's marital success: sex on Sundays. No matter what, he and his spouse devote their Sunday mornings to a routine that involves breakfast, a walk, and sex—sometimes not in that order. They have come to rely on this routine. Although scheduling sexual activity doesn't sound all that sexy because it's not spontaneous, it is a highly effective strategy for staying sexually connected, and the anticipation of knowing they have some sexy time planned together can actually intensify the experience for couples. For new parents, we can't overestimate how important it is to set up these routines now, as well as to find more extended times together (e.g., a weekend away, just the two of you, while Auntie watches the kids).

Couple: Karlee and Anderson

Prescription: Relationship Medicine: Declare a Truce and Establish Rules of Engagement; Alternate Date Night; Bonus: Visit to Fantasy Island

Compared to Benito and Ariana's, Karlee and Anderson's struggles were a bit more complex. As their problems had magnified over the years, they had become really angry at each other, and sex (and physical affection) had become one of their primary battlefields. While make-up sex has a mythic reputation as being intense and sexier than sex that doesn't follow a fight, the fact is that for most couples, sex is incompatible with *ongoing or more deep-seated anger*, and so, for the most part, is desire. Yes, sex can be an effective way to reconnect after there has been a fight or an argument, but it should not be the go-to solution or become a pattern for all that ails a couple. When problems are more long-standing, even if sex happens, the quality of sex is going to be marginal to off-putting since those deeper feelings of resentment corrode perception of the other person. Anger and resentment cut off the ways a couple might move toward each other in reconciliation and affection. This can be expressed as avoidance of each other, moving out of the bedroom, or feeling that the other person's touch is unsafe or unwanted. Karlee and Anderson had been steadily reducing the rewards of marriage for themselves and each other, so this relationship was on a downward trajectory if the root of this anger was not discovered, addressed, and replaced with more understanding and emotional connection.

Declare a Truce and Establish Rules of Engagement

So the exercise here was to declare a truce and then create a plan to communicate better, which included each of them writing down what was really bothering them about the other person and the marriage. This was difficult to do and to hear, so it also required creating *rules of engagement* about how this problem would be shared and discussed.

Rules of engagement for couples can include the following:

- We will be honest but not cruel.
- No name-calling. No shaming.
- Our goal will be to resolve this so we can move forward.
- No leaving the conversation, but it's okay to ask for a twenty-minute break.
- Assume that we both want the same things—to connect and to improve our relationship.
- We will take the stance of "it's you and me against the problem, not you against me."
- We will try to use "I feel" statements instead of blaming each other.
- We will state positive needs (e.g., "I need to feel closer to you, and one way we could do that is to plan more time for physical or sexual connection").

This will require brutal honesty but not cruelty. There is a difference, and it is critical that both parties agree that the rules of engagement include tact as well as truth. As it turned out in this case, the issue was about respect and communication. When Karlee wrote down her complaints, she realized that she used moving out of the bedroom as a way of having some control over the conversations and, truth be told, as punishment for Anderson's lack of respect for her opinion. Anderson had no idea what was causing the anger; he thought she had to have her way all the time and they just naturally were butting heads and were basically incompatible. When he heard her say she felt unimportant to him, he said he would try to listen more. It became very clear that when they could each give the other time for their opinions to be fully stated and then ask questions about those opinions, as opposed to just insisting on their own opinions (or leaving the scene and going to another bedroom), softer feelings had time to surface. And with warmer feelings, sexual desire started to return.

Alternate Date Night

The second dose of medicine for this couple was for them to reinstate their date nights and be sure to do them at least weekly. One strategy we love to prescribe for couples is to alternate date nights, in which they take turns picking the activity, venue, or outing for the date. To take it to the next level, they could consider adding an extra dose of Vitamins: a Visit to Fantasy Island. Karlee and Anderson, both recognizing that they had long ago given up regular date nights, agreed to a plan of restarting date nights—once per week, they would try a different place or activity together, and they began to look forward in anticipation to what was in store for them. Karlee had always wanted to try roller-blading, and they had a blast trying, laughing, and falling repeatedly together. Anderson took Karlee to a Vietnamese cooking class, and they both enjoyed it so much that their next date night was at home trying the recipes they learned together. Reconnecting through activities, play, and laughter made them feel more connected, which translated into increased interest in the bedroom—where they then decided to follow our suggestion to try out the Visit to Fantasy Island activity.

Visit to Fantasy Island

This is a fun (and sexy!) exercise that might benefit both of the couples we've mentioned—from our new parents who needed to be reminded that they were sexual beings, not just parents, to our couple who was struggling to reconnect sexually and needed something they could bond over in the bedroom. When couples try this activity, they are challenged with writing down their top three sexual fantasies and then sharing them with their partners. A few ground rules: Listen to your partner's fantasies without being offended—we all have different fantasies and turn-ons and want to create a space where we can feel free to share without feeling judged. We encourage couples to have open minds and approach this exercise with a sense of fun and adventure. Talk about how you could make each fantasy a reality. At the same time, since this may be outside your comfort zone, we want to emphasize that *nobody should do something that makes them feel uncomfortable or ashamed or something they do not want to do.*

How did this process work for Karlee and Anderson? Before getting ready for one of their date nights to a local restaurant, they took fifteen to thirty minutes to write down their fantasies, keeping those ground rules in mind. Karlee wrote about how she wanted to experiment more with toys but wasn't sure how to bring this idea up to Anderson without implying that he wasn't satisfying her; she also discussed that she had an ongoing fantasy about an intense massage with a sexy masseur that would lead to passionate sex. Anderson wrote that he always fantasized about having his lover dominate him and take control. He also wrote about a fantasy he had of having a threesome with his wife and another (unnamed) woman. They shared their fantasies over drinks at dinner, and the conversation became so intense, they barely made it home! Karlee thanked Anderson for sharing about his desire for a threesome but told him that she did not feel comfortable with this suggestion, saying, "I'm too possessive." Anderson laughed and said he didn't either in reality. Ultimately, they both agreed that they were uncomfortable with a threesome, but Karlee agreed to talk about threesomes while having sex, which in and of itself was hot to Anderson. On a subsequent date night, they planned a trip to an adult store, where they were able to find a few items (e.g., sex toys, massage oil, and a play whip) they could use to potentially meet each other's fantasies. While not every tryst they had between the sheets was a fantasy fulfilled, being more open, communicating about their desires and what felt good and not good, and experimenting with each other led to their sex increasing in frequency and more so in quality and connection.

Couple: Glenn and Bernard

Prescription: Relationship CPR: Couples Therapy; Individual Therapy for Treatment of Sex Addiction

Given the gravity of the infidelity, potential porn addiction, and vast disagreement about consensual monogamy, Bernard and Glenn were far past a Relationship Vitamins or Medicine solution. Had they had the opportunity earlier in their relationship to sharpen their communication with a goal to stay on the same page for the sake of their relationship, they may have been able to avoid the pain and now-dire circumstances.

A serious difference of opinion about monogamy is usually a big problem because it brings up primal feelings and primal angers, by which we mean very core feelings about being special, loved, loved enough, and desired enough. Often there is almost a species-wide feeling of territory that has been invaded: "That spouse's body *is mine!*" The pair bond is one of the more unique features of human mating relationships. However, contrary to what one may think, having more sexual partners does not equate to more happiness. When surveying adults about the number of partners they have had in the previous year, the number that maximized happiness was one.[3]

Now, there are exceptions. If both people can work out a plan for having outside sexual experiences, the relationship can be managed within the context of open communication and clear boundaries. There are couples who can tell very convincing stories about why those experiences don't hurt their primary relationship. However, even that brings up its own issues, particularly if one or both partners get attached to someone else.

But if there is disagreement about whether monogamy is required (as in the example of Glenn and Bernard), if there are different emotional values and needs, the problem escalates to explosive pretty quickly. Most (though not all) people have powerful feelings of jealousy and emotional insecurity in general, and even more so when it comes to their lovers or spouses. If they love their partners, even seeing their spouses give a lot of attention to other people (much less sexual contact) naturally arouses some degree of fear, anger, or anxiety over possible abandonment, impending loss, or self-doubt. This tendency is even higher for those who have an anxious attachment style. If their partners express desire to have open relationships, they are likely to feel this suggestion is a violation of their partners' loyalty and a gateway to ending the relationships. For many religious or devout people, it is breaking a sacred vow that they made to God, as well as to each other.

The gay male world is made up of men with a variety of opinions, religious backgrounds, values, and opinions, but there are undisputedly more gay men who feel that monogamy is a heterosexual norm and not suitable for men in general and gay men in particular—so Glenn's wish for non-monogamy is not necessarily shocking given the cultural context. While not all gay men believe in or practice non-monogamy, research suggests that 30–40 percent of gay men do practice non-monogamy and have more open relationships in which there is an agreement that they can be sexually intimate with others.[4] There is a large group of gay men who believe that monogamy is unnatural, sex can just be recreational fun, and sex with others will not harm their committed relationships. Sometimes both partners feel this way, and they can enjoy sex with other people and still come home at night to a happy partner. But it would be misleading to think all gay men are like this, and Bernard certainly was not. He came from a religious background, and their wedding vows (done in church) included the phrase "forsaking all others," and he meant it. He thought Glenn meant it too, and when Glenn said that he found monogamy too constricting, Bernard tried to change his feelings about sex outside their marriage, but he could not. He was angry all the time and despondent when Glenn would have crushes, even though they had all turned out to be fleeting, and he felt terrible that Glenn took so much time away from the relationship. He decided that even though they had had a wonderful relationship and marriage in so many ways, he was done.

When one partner thinks they are done, we are in the CPR category. And, like actual CPR, time may be of the essence. We suggest going to see a skilled therapist with expertise in both sexuality and addiction. Of course, in the case of Glenn and Bernard, it would have been better to deal with this difference of values and behavior about sex outside the relationship before Glenn embarked on this new approach to their relationship—perhaps with a more Vitamins-level approach exploring their attachment styles and practicing using reflective listening in their early years together. But since that horse is out of the barn and now running from pasture to greener pastures, a series of questions to ask the therapist and topics to address could be very helpful.

First, how committed to the relationship is the partner who is looking for outside sex? If he or she is really not committed to the relationship, there is really nothing to talk about. But in this case, Glenn really loves Bernard, doesn't want to hurt him, and doesn't want to break up the relationship, so there is a chance for repair. Adding insult to injury, however, is Bernard's revelation that Glenn may be addicted to Internet porn, and this issue will have to be carefully unpacked with a therapist skilled in addressing sex addiction. Glenn and Bernard will want to inquire as to whether the same therapist could provide some assessment or insight into sex addiction and treatment options or make a referral to another specialist.

A therapist will dig deep to find out why non-monogamy is so important to Glenn, especially given that it endangers a longtime relationship. Sometimes getting to the bottom of the behavior can uncover a compulsive set of behaviors that could be changed or modified. Given that Glenn spends hours per day looking at porn, it is likely that there is an addictive component at play here. If it's revealed that in fact Glenn is struggling with addiction, and if Glenn is unable or unwilling to take steps to address this problem in treatment, there really is no point in this relationship continuing. At the same time, the therapist might find that it is not sex that the non-monogamous partner yearns for but adventure, reassurance of his or her own sexual vitality, or perhaps there is a fear of true secure attachment. If, for example, a spouse needs other partners as a pattern of need for constant reassurance that he or she is attractive or special, individual counseling might be able to modify the situation by exploring where those needs actually come from. Getting to the origins of the need might make it possible to change the outside roaming (though that result is certainly not guaranteed). Bernard may also benefit from working with his own individual therapist to discuss the impact of Glenn's infidelity on his self-worth and process his own thoughts related to monogamy versus non-monogamy, as well as explore his patterns of continuing to forgive Glenn and excuse the behavior in the past at his own expense. In any case, Glenn and Bernard have a long road ahead of them—but if they both truly want this marriage to continue (and not be miserable) and they both put in the work, they might find themselves in a relationship in which each is ultimately happier and fulfilled.

Summary

Attraction is what often brings us to our partners in the first place, and sex is a connection that couples have over any other important relationship. A satisfying, healthy sex life has dramatic impacts on our physical health, stress levels, mental health, and overall life satisfaction. And, as we mentioned, sex is a good barometer for the rest of our relationship—if our sex lives are tanking, chances are that other areas are in trouble too. Remember, for most people, true sexual intimacy cannot be fully realized until we are able to better master emotional intimacy (see chapter 3). Having solid communication, trust, and respect for our partners can dramatically improve how we operate between the sheets—resulting in increased confidence in ourselves and in our relationships and increased overall satisfaction. At the same time, what works for one couple may not for another, so don't compare yourselves to your neighbors, and make sure you're establishing boundaries and building a sex life that works for the two of you. With the right tools and strategies, you can negotiate a sex life that you are both happy with. At the end of the day, you know your lives best, and if you can put your egos aside and put your brains together, you can come up with a sexy plan that works for both of you.

5

UNMET EXPECTATIONS AND UNFULFILLED NEEDS

My husband is supposed to be my best friend. This isn't what I thought marriage would be like. My partner has changed. He was so adventurous before and now he's boring. We used to be together 24-7, but now he's spending time with everything and everyone except me.

A famous quote, attributed to William Shakespeare: "Expectation is the root of all heartache." Unmet expectations in relationships are common—so common that research has suggested that when asked about whether unmet expectations contributed to divorce, almost 50 percent of people said that their unmet expectations or those of their partners were a major contributor to the demise of their marriages.[1] Think about it. Sex, money, kids, division of labor—much of this comes down to conflict between what we expect and what we actually get.

There's nothing wrong with expectations. Our expectations, or beliefs about the way things or people should operate, are informed by societal expectations and our own histories. There are expectations that are reasonable—expecting that our partners are there to support us through happy and difficult times for better or worse, that they will stay faithful, and that we are both in this together. However, even reasonable expectations can bring disappointments.

We've had expectations drilled into our minds since listening to our first fairy tales or watching our first Disney movies. Our beloveds are supposed to show up on a horse, swing in from the trees, or emerge from the ocean, and with their kisses, all is right in the world, all our problems are solved, and we live happily ever after (with beautiful clothes and perfectly coiffed hair). In today's day and age, expectations of relationships and each other are even further distorted by overly curated Instagram and TikTok feeds of ideal relationships.

There are some expectations that many have that really are what we call "cognitive distortions"—thoughts that we have that are inaccurate or just not helpful. Here are some examples:

- He/She/They should complete me.
- Once we're married, everything will be perfect.
- My partner will never change.
- Marriage shouldn't be difficult.
- I can change him/her/them how I want to.
- Our sex life will always be consistently great.
- My spouse's job is to make me a better (smarter, kinder, more driven, etc.) person.
- He'll give me what I want all the time because he loves me.
- We should never go to bed angry or in the middle of an argument.
- Her life should revolve around mine.
- We should spend all our free time together.

Any of these thoughts sound familiar? What they all have in common is that they are either inaccurate or unhelpful ways of thinking. They are thoughts that can erode even the happiest of relationships.

The hard truth is that even Prince Charming has dirty dishes that need to be done. And both he and his blushing bride will disappoint each other multiple times throughout their fairy-tale romance. Whether realistic or not, your expectations will inevitably be unmet at some point, your needs will be unfulfilled, and you will be disappointed. That's part of being human and part of any long-term relationship. Disappointment, however, can lead to resentment and frustration, which can lead to anger and ultimately to a partner withdrawing or punishing the other. What's difficult to grasp about this original disappointment is that you—*and your expectations and how you handle them*—are part of the problem.

Let's take a look at three couples, each struggling with issues related to their unmet expectations and unfulfilled needs.

Couple #1: Leo and Melissa: Mild Relationship Symptoms Related to Unfulfilled Needs and Unmet Expectations

Leo and Melissa are newlyweds in their first year of marriage. When dating, they couldn't get enough of each other, would stay up talking and laughing until late into the evening, and were the best of friends. Melissa became pregnant five months ago, and Leo has been feeling like Melissa isn't as interested in him as she was before. Leo has been feeling starved for attention, and Melissa is feeling irritated that Leo hasn't been stepping up more around the house. Melissa is getting worried about how frustrated with her Leo may be after the baby is born and she can't give him the attention he wants.

Couple #2: Antonio and Andrea: Moderate Relationship Symptoms Related to Unfulfilled Needs and Unmet Expectations

Antonio and Andrea have been married for six years but together for nine. In their early years, they spent every waking (and sleeping) minute together—Andrea described Antonio as "the man of my dreams," and Antonio loved the nonstop attention that Andrea poured on him. In the last year or more, they have hit some major barriers in their relationship. Antonio started spending longer hours at work, hanging out with his colleagues after hours, and playing golf much of the weekend. Andrea is lonely and disappointed; Antonio feels defensive and like Andrea is constantly "on me." Their text exchanges during the week are short, their sex life is lackluster, and both of them occasionally wonder whether they would be happier in other relationships or on their own.

Couple #3: Will and Cara: Severe Relationship Symptoms Related to Unfulfilled Needs and Unmet Expectations

Will and Cara have been married for eighteen years and have four children together. After a number of ups and downs in their marriage, they have hit a crisis point. Will has been having what he says is an emotional affair with one of their friends, spending much of his time talking and texting with this other woman. Cara, angry with Will for what she believes is worse than him cheating on her (which he did very early on in their marriage), has been flirting heavily with her coworkers and her personal trainer—and had a one-night stand on a recent work trip at a conference.

All three couples have in common disappointment related to how they expected their relationship to be. Over time, the gloss faded on the picture-perfect relationship and they realized that their hopes were less than fulfilled and that their partners failed to be the partners they thought they would be. Each of these couples has allowed the individual thoughts and beliefs they had about marriage to impact the feelings they have about their current unions. Disappointment has led to hurt, hurt has led to anger, and anger, for some, has led to punishing their spouses or icing them out completely.

Yes, it's an amazing feeling when our partners can take care of us and fulfill our needs. There should absolutely be times in our relationships when that's the case. However, no human being is capable of meeting (or willing to meet) all our needs and their own needs all the time. While it's OK to be dependent on one another when we need to be, if we're dependent on one person to meet all our needs, neither we nor our partners will be happy because it's simply not sustainable in the long run.

So maybe you've been told your expectations are too high. There are going to be some relationship experts who tell you to lower your expectations. We aren't those experts. There's nothing wrong with having high (but realistic) expectations! In fact, research has shown when people have high expectations—for themselves and each other—they tend to be in relationships in which they are treated well.[2] By having higher expectations, people are more likely to have the types of relationships they want—with the caveat being that they do not expect their relationships to be conflict free. We aren't saying you should aim for having a perfect relationship. In a sense, we're striving for what Drs. John and Julie Gottman call a "good enough" relationship—one in which we have high expectations for ourselves and each other, such as affection, respect, loyalty, and kindness.[3] At the same time, while not tolerating abusive behavior or settling for being treated poorly, couples in good-enough relationships know that conflict is a natural, healthy part of a relationship and a way in which partners can deepen their understanding of each other.

One fairly common expectation in relationships that couples can work on adjusting: expecting that they will solve all the problems in their relationships. Relationship science, with many studies from the mid-1990s from Gottman's "Love Lab,"[4] has shown us that almost two-thirds of relationship conflict is perpetual—that we will likely have the same arguments over the same problems throughout the relationship. Some problems are just unsolvable (e.g., when couples parent differently, don't agree about politics, or have different temperaments), and couples do better when they can accept their differences. Accept that some problems are just not solvable, and that's OK!

Both our expectations and our needs can be unmet or unfulfilled in our relationships. We want to emphasize that expectations are different from needs. An expectation is a thought we tell ourselves or what we believe, such as "My partner needs to have dinner ready for me when I come home" or "My partner should know how I feel." A need is internal and personal, but needs are also universal feelings: "I need to feel appreciated. I need to feel loved. I need to feel special. I need to feel safe and secure in my relationship." Often, our expectations are related to our needs. For example, "My partner should have dinner ready for me when I get home" may actually be related to "I need to feel appreciated and special—I feel appreciated and special when my partner prepares a meal for me after I've had a long day."

There are some ways we can adjust how we think and ultimately improve our relationships and our satisfaction in them (similar to our Cognitive Triangle exercise in chapter 2). Here are examples of thoughts or expectations that won't lead to frustrations:

- My partner is human and we both make mistakes.
- Our marriage isn't perfect, but it's good enough.
- Things are tough right now, but this is a challenge for us to overcome together.
- It's you and me versus the problem.
- Not all of our problems can be solved and that's OK.
- I expect to be treated with kindness.
- I expect my partner to be loyal to me, and I expect myself to be loyal to my partner.

- My partner has needs too. Sometimes my partner's needs aren't the same as mine, and that's OK.

Let's do a closer examination of our couples.

Leo and Melissa: Mild Relationship Symptoms Related to Unfulfilled Needs and Unmet Expectations

Leo and Melissa fell in love after meeting on a dating app—they both thought the other person "was even better in person" than on the dating profiles, and within weeks they declared that they were soul mates. After Melissa became pregnant, she had a terrible first trimester during which everything made her nauseous and all she could do was think about sleep. Although they both planned to have children, the pregnancy was a bit of a surprise and both of them wish they had more time to be married, just the two of them. Melissa is nervous about being a mother and about how she is going to handle all the responsibilities of working and parenting, but she is too tired to talk to Leo about how she feels and he seems "just not that interested" in her pregnancy. She says, "I thought he wanted to have children. I know I'm carrying the baby, but I figured we'd be in this together! . . . I feel like so much is happening to me and he doesn't even care." At the same time, Leo says that Melissa is preoccupied and distracted all the time, and "I feel bad that she's been feeling sick and tired, but I just try to take her mind off of it." Leo, missing the attention Melissa normally gave him, including what was a healthy and active sex life, says that he has been feeling bored but also knows that they will be busy with a baby in a few months. Leo says, "I love how adventurous she used to be—she used to be up for anything. But when I ask her what she wants to do, all she wants to do is stay home." Leo believes that every time he talks to her, she seems "irritated with me—like nothing I do is right."

Antonio and Andrea: Moderate Relationship Symptoms Related to Unfulfilled Needs and Unmet Expectations

In their early years, Andrea would describe Antonio as her knight in shining armor and she was drawn to Antonio's protective qualities. She loved being his wife—nothing seemed to bring her more satisfaction than taking care of her husband. Antonio loved how doting his wife was, and although he saw himself as a progressive thinker when it came to relationships, he grew up in a home where masculinity was defined by how much money a man could bring home and femininity was defined by how well a woman cooked and took care of herself. As work demands increased, he began spending more time at the office, and sometimes it was just easier to finish a work meeting with coworkers at dinner before heading home or to talk things out over drinks. Explaining that his work life was stressful and he needed more ways to blow off steam, he was able to unwind on the golf course—but golf games took time, and he usually needed a nap afterward. He vehemently denied having any sort of extramarital affair but did acknowledge that he had been spending far less time at home than he used to, and when he did come home, it seemed like Andrea was consistently disappointed and needy or really clingy. He expected Andrea to realize that he needed to relieve stress, saying, "She should know how stressful my work is. She's known me long enough to know that I don't like to be nagged and I need time to chill out." He adds, "Everything I do at work is to build a life for us. I bring her flowers, I buy her the bags she wants. Why isn't that good enough?"

Andrea feels like Antonio has been pulling away for some time—and this leaves her feeling anxious. She says, "It's like I just walk around in circles in our house" and "I've never been lonelier." Andrea, who has defined her identity as Antonio's wife, had relinquished most of her interests, hobbies, and friendships when she entered her marriage to Antonio because "nothing made me happier." However, the void—the silence—that surrounds her when he is not there is suffocating and sad, leaving her to question who she is and what her purpose is. Andrea has become increasingly upset when Antonio talks to her about something that he previously confided in a coworker or one of his siblings. She says, "It's like now I'm the last to know." Andrea expects Antonio to spend all his free time with her; her need for emotional and social connections is vastly unfulfilled. Over time, her sadness has turned to anger, her mood is generally irritable, and her behavior toward Antonio is passive-aggressive. Antonio feels stressed and annoyed by her behavior, saying, "No matter what I do, it's not good enough."

Will and Cara: Severe Relationship Symptoms Related to Unfulfilled Needs and Unmet Expectations

Both Will and Cara are unsure when their marriage hit a dead end, but the bottom line is that they are absolutely miserable. Their relationship has been a roller coaster of volatility—and they've been together since their college years—but what has always kept them together has been their belief that their children are better off if they keep their marriage intact. They each expected that they would put their family first. Will had an affair early in their marriage, when Cara was pregnant with their first child. After working with a pastoral counselor at the time, they agreed to make their marriage work. Cara admitted recently that she never really got over that betrayal, and the disappointment and pain she felt from Will's affair diminished but never went away. "It changed us," she said. Will claims that this was the only time he has physically stepped out on their marriage—but in the last eighteen months, he has reconnected with one of their former college friends on Facebook, Mandy, who was also unhappily married. Will, relishing the attention Mandy gave him, says things like "She actually listens to me" and "She values what I have to say." He looked forward to his conversations with Mandy and even acknowledges that he would have butterflies when he had a text message from her. He began confiding all sorts of things in Mandy—his dreams, his disappointments, and his challenges in his marriage. Mandy, too, shared with him that she was in a marriage that had gotten stale.

Although Cara knew Will and Mandy were talking, she did not realize the extent of their communication until she saw their cell phone bill and realized that they had spoken almost every day in the last year and a half—and the number of text messages was in the thousands. Cara acknowledges how painful this revelation was for her: "My husband was supposed to be my best friend, not some other woman's! He talks to her about everything, when all I get is a three-word text reminding me to take out the trash." It has been not weeks but months since they have had sex. In the meantime, Cara, desperate to connect with someone and to know that she is desirable and worthy, has been flirting heavily with her coworkers and her personal trainer. Although Will does not know, she had a one-night stand on a recent work trip at a conference and says, "I didn't even feel bad about it—it made me feel like I was alive again."

It's not unreasonable for Cara to expect Will to be faithful to her. Just because she expects it, though, doesn't mean he is going to follow through. In order to move through the turmoil and pain of an affair, it can be helpful to shift from "*he shouldn't have* cheated" to "*I wish he wouldn't have* cheated." This shift can allow us to move past the anger and through the healthy grief that follows.

RELATIONSHIP Rx FOR EACH COUPLE

Couple: Leo and Melissa

Prescription: Relationship Vitamins: "One Night Out and One Night In" Coupled with a "How I Want to Feel" Exercise

"One Night Out and One Night In"

Leo and Melissa could benefit from what we call "One Night Out and One Night In" each week. The idea is that couples prioritize a date night, but on the night out, they follow strict rules not to talk about kids or, in Leo and Melissa's case, the pregnancy and new baby coming. They were challenged with finding a new place for dinner or a new activity—to increase the opportunity for conversation and connection but also for a bit more adventure. On their one night in, they planned a meal together or a task, such as painting the baby's room or putting together a crib. For their one night in, they were charged with talking about their plans for the future, Melissa's pregnancy, and topics related to their growing family. Having these boundaries allowed for protected time for romance (and, for Leo, that adventure that he loved in his wife), as well as protected time for Melissa to feel Leo's support of her during her pregnancy and for him to support her worries related to their future.

"How I Want to Feel"

For this strategy, we suggest that couples list on a small piece of paper how they want to feel in their relationships (which could be put on the mirror or in one's wallet). This list will vary from person to person but could include feelings such as "desired," "secure," "loved," and "valued." Make a copy of your list and share it with your partner. In doing so, ask each other, "What do you need from me in order to feel that way?" and "What are things that I could do or we could do together to help you feel that way?" Each of you should keep your list somewhere close so you can refer to it and even add to it over time.

Couple: Antonio and Andrea

Prescription: Relationship Medicine: Expectations Not Frustrations; Me Time, You Time

Expectations Not Frustrations

Andrea and Antonio could benefit from trying the Expectations Not Frustrations exercise. First, take a piece of paper and write down what expectations you currently have for yourself, your partner, and your relationship. After you've taken the time to write down your answers, think about how each expectation may actually be tied to a need. Then write down what those needs are. For example, one might have the expectation that his or her partner should hug and kiss them when the partner comes home from work, but the need may be "I need physical connection from my partner after we have been apart in order to feel loved." After you have been able to clarify the need, sit down with your partner to share both your expectations and your needs. There may be some needs on your list that are not possible for your partner to fulfill all the time. This is where you may need to brainstorm alternative ways to meet those needs.

Andrea wrote down that she expected herself to prioritize her husband over everything and was able to clarify that this need for her was "to feel valued and loved." She expected Antonio to have dinner with her most days of the week. She then clarified for herself that it wasn't the dinner that was important, but rather that "I need to feel important to my husband" and that having dinner together showed her that she and their family were a priority. Antonio wrote down that he expected himself to be the provider for his family and that this expectation was tied to his own need of "I need to feel successful; I need to feel that I have value." He wrote that he expected Andrea to "know what I need and to know that I love her even when we're not together," but his need was "to have some independence."

When they shared their lists, they quickly realized that they both needed to feel valued, but they achieved this result from each other and their relationship in different ways. Andrea felt her value the most when she was able to take care of Antonio and spend time with him. But as he spent more time fulfilling his need to feel valued by working longer and with other people, she was not able to get her need met. Andrea was able to recognize that her identity had been wrapped up so much in being Antonio's wife that she had prioritized him over even herself. In Andrea's case, it's not that she was "needy," as Antonio had claimed she was—she just wasn't getting what she needed.

Me Time, You Time

Andrea realized that the void in her life that she felt when Antonio was not home was not just because of his absence but also because of her no longer having interests, relationships, and time with herself. They agreed to a Me Time, You Time strategy in which, at least two days per week, they would each do activities of their own choosing. Antonio prioritized his golf games, while Andrea was encouraged to think about hobbies or interests that made her happy. Andrea, who used to paint, picked up a brush and canvases and spent time painting on her own. She had forgotten how much she enjoyed painting and how cathartic it was for her. She then got in touch with friends she had lost contact with, and they joined a bimonthly paint-and-sip class, which she enjoyed. She also joined a local yoga studio and met friends for yoga at least once per week. Through these new activities, Andrea was able to meet her need for connection, which helped her feel better about herself. When she was with Antonio, she was reenergized, and this time apart actually strengthened their connection in that they had more to share with each other.

Couple: Will and Cara

Prescription: Relationship CPR: Couples Therapy

Will and Cara hit a crisis point long ago in their marriage—and at this point, drastic measures need to be taken. Working with a couples therapist, they will need to unpack whether they believe the marriage is worth saving. In therapy, they can explore the expectations they had about their marriage and each other, as well as identify the needs that have not been met. In couples therapy, they will benefit from exploring how their relationship shifted with Will's early infidelity in the marriage. Should they move forward, both partners will need to put the work in. It is highly likely that Will may have to put some serious boundaries with Mandy in place—and even make the decision to end their communication if he decides that he wants to save his marriage.

Summary

Even in the greatest of love stories, couples are going to bicker about laundry and have a moment when they miss their early dating years. This is normal. It's OK to have high expectations, as long as those expectations are realistic. Even Prince Charming is going to forget to put his coffee mug in the sink. Even the fairest of princesses will have days when she is a hot mess. Couples will not be on the same page 100 percent of the time. Couples will disappoint each other. However, if couples are provided the right tools and strategies to communicate about their expectations, they are likely to have a greater understanding of their partners' expectations and their own. Often, the unmet expectation is actually more related to an unfulfilled need. And, as we mentioned, couples do well when they reach the point of recognizing that some problems (e.g., the same argument you have over and over and over) are not going to be fully solved. Couples who are happy and successful (most of the time) strive for good-enough relationships—in which they are good friends, are committed to each other, have a decent sex life, trust each other, and know how to fight and how to apologize when they have hurt each other. They appreciate the ways they are different. When conflict arises due to unmet expectations or unfulfilled needs, they can work through it in order to either arrive at an effective compromise or understand that perhaps this problem can't be solved, but they can come to an acceptance or let go of the tension related to it.

6

BOREDOM

Our relationship just isn't fun anymore. It feels like the same thing every day. Doesn't everyone complain that their marriage is boring? He used to be so adventurous. She was up for anything. Are other couples this bored? We seem to fight just to avoid things being dull.

Here's the hard truth about marriage or a lifetime relationship by any other name: It is not an affair. Without the longing and uncertainty of the other person's love, or without the newness of a first kiss or the first "I love you" and those precious months, maybe even years, of passion and sexual euphoria, even the greatest of relationships will settle into a pattern. And patterns are soothing and familiar and a profile of the life you have built together—so, so far, so good. But patterns can also be boring. Think of steak for breakfast, lunch, and dinner . . . every single day. After a long period of time, well, you might fantasize about going vegan. Still, no matter what we know with our rational minds about the impact of habituation (i.e., the psychology behind "getting used to it") on our sexual desire and our emotional connections, no one promises to settle for an eventually boring marriage when they say their vows. At the altar, we are full of hope, deep attraction, and fluttery feelings, with our minds focused on our dreams and fantasies about the life ahead of us. "Boring" seems unimaginable. Fifteen years later, however, if someone asks whether one's marriage is ever boring, most people will say, "Of course. Isn't everyone's?"

Well, not everyone's. Some people try to keep their relationships from being boring by having tumultuous periods every so often, marked by major blowups or bad behavior by one or both parties: threatening to leave, getting mad at each other, breaking up for a while, having an affair, or, less damaging, traveling to a new country every month and battling travel's inevitable challenges. In fact, there are ways to combat the same old, same old—even volatile ways, which we don't recommend. When faced with the inevitable entrance of boredom, the first thing is that we have to recognize that the same old, same old has arrived and, second, be willing to do something about it. And that something, ideally, doesn't include having a tryst with a coworker or surrendering to the boredom and working later hours at the office.

We are here to tell you that marriage can be fun. Marriage can be inventive, sexy, and adventurous—marriage can be the thing you are most grateful for in your life. But rarely does it offer all of that unless a mindful, intentional approach is taken to gauge its daily or weekly temperature and appropriate steps are taken when the dullness or even sadness enters the scene.

Here are some couples on the edge or deep in the weeds whose marriages are (or are becoming) inert.

Couple #1: Celeste and D'Andra: Mild Relationship Symptoms Related to Boredom

Both Celeste and D'Andra, together for twenty-one years, have always been content being homebodies. They have a blended family with adult children and have settled into a very predictable routine over the years. Lately, Celeste has been feeling restless, and D'Andra feels like Celeste has been pulling away and wonders whether she is depressed.

Couple #2: Phil and Georgia: Moderate Relationship Symptoms Related to Boredom

Phil and Georgia, married six years, had a relationship marked by adventure and excitement—traveling together all over the world—until they had kids. They now have two children under age five. Phil continues to crave adventure and has been taking trips on his own, but Georgia is too exhausted to do much of anything and doesn't want to leave the children, so she stays home. Phil is frustrated and lonely; Georgia is also frustrated and lonely.

Couple #3: Samantha and Carl: Severe Relationship Symptoms Related to Boredom

Samantha and Carl have been together for fourteen years. Lately, their troubles have become serious. Carl has been avoiding Samantha's company, except when they go out with other people. When they are with others, each of them trades nasty jabs about the other in a way that is embarrassing and even humiliating. They barely speak to each other at home, and tensions have been high for months.

All three of these couples are faced with something so many couples will experience—the time when the excitement of falling in love decreases and we become comfortable, content, and then, over time, bored and even restless. This boredom and associated feelings of sadness or annoyance or longing for a different life can be avoided as long as couples are willing to do the work in recognizing that there is value in what we believe is boring or routine and that there are measures we can take to prevent feeling bored in our relationships.

When we are falling in love, we feel "chemistry"—our hearts pound around that person, we have butterflies, we are excited and filled with anticipation at just seeing them or hearing their voice or seeing a text pop up. During this phase, we are filled with hormones; many of these are actually stress hormones that engage us to pursue the one we love, which might explain that tunnel vision we see in couples who are falling in love. The problem is that when those stress hormones (e.g., cortisol) are high and the prefrontal cortex is less engaged, we may overlook our loved one's flaws or shortcomings. Over time, stress hormones decrease and mood-regulating hormones (e.g., serotonin) are stabilized, and we feel more comfortable than excited when we are with our partner. We see more of their good side, as well as the other side. Long story short, the flip side to feeling secure and comfortable in a relationship is boredom.

Relationships will fall into patterns, and routines and will get predictable. One thing we caution couples about is paying attention to specific thinking they may have or language they may use when this happens. Is the relationship "boring" or "mundane"? Or, taking a gentler approach, is it "secure" and "dependable"? Remember chapter 2, where we talk about how predictability and rituals and routines with couples can strengthen their connection and actually promote secure attachment? Boredom doesn't happen just because we're repeating the same routines—it's because we aren't satisfied with those routines, which is why having gratitude for what "boring" actually brings us can increase our satisfaction with the relationship we have.

Look, nobody is immune to wanting to spice things up in their lives now and then. We all want some degree of excitement as well as security. Some people are natural-born thrill seekers or sensation seekers—and those who are far on this spectrum (e.g., those with attention deficit hyperactivity disorder, or AD/HD) may struggle with more intense boredom in multiple facets of their lives. (FYI: For those with true AD/HD, we recommend working with someone who specializes in this condition to help them meet their needs without sabotaging their relationships.) The problem is that when we act on the desire to shake things up without thinking it through, that impulsive act or spontaneous behavior may lead us to end up more dissatisfied than we were at the start. There is value in predictability; there is comfort in routine and dependability.

In chapter 3, we talk about a study in which couples who had been together for many, many years were still describing themselves as being deeply in love with their partners. This study compared the brains of couples who had been together for different lengths of time. The researchers compared brain scans and found that there were no differences in the intensity of activity in dopamine-rich areas of the brain—demonstrating that a long-term relationship doesn't equal boredom, nor does it have to decrease the romance. Just because we might be bored doesn't mean we need to change our partners. It just means we need to try a different approach. Keep in mind that the comfort, security, and support of a long-term relationship can actually afford us special benefits that our single counterparts may not have—we and our partners can take turns supporting each other on new career paths or other adventures or risks. When our marriages or our relationships are the foundations from which we can grow and experiment in life, there is no room to be bored!

OK, so even though you may know that stability and predictability are good for you in a relationship, you're still feeling bored? Here's another hard truth: *The reason your relationship is boring may be your own fault.*

You have to work to keep that love brain working overtime. The brain stops working as hard once something becomes routine or normal in order to save energy for more complex cognitive tasks—which may partially explain why we sometimes take our closest relationships for granted. How can you increase that dopamine or those other feel-good chemicals and continue to keep your relationship passionate and alive? There are a number of ways, and here are just a few suggestions:

1. Write down or tell your partner how much you appreciate him or her and what you love about him or her. Thank your partner for doing things for you or for things you might take for granted (e.g., bringing coffee in the morning, rubbing your feet at night, or getting up with the kids so you can sleep). Give little gifts or tokens of affection or appreciation. Praise and positive reinforcement are Psychology 101—when you praise or "reward" your partner, dopamine is released (for both of you) and your partner is more likely to keep doing the things you like. It sounds basic, but it is very effective.

2. Use the element of surprise—whether it be an unexpected "I love you" text (or something sexier) instead of the "What do you need at the store?" text, a surprise date to an unknown location, or a gift just because. What better way to bust out of a rut or routine than by doing something that surprises your significant other? Sometimes it's the unexpectedness or the spontaneity that your partner is wanting. Offering an unexpected gesture may result in those feelings of excitement or anticipation you had earlier in your relationship.

3. Focus on your appearance. One thing that happens with all couples is we stop trying as hard to be physically attractive to our spouses. Think about when you first started dating, with your hair done, nails done, and best outfit or cologne and the shirt that made your eyes pop. Over time, we sometimes settle into the "sweatpants, messy bun, no bra" routine, which can be sexy in its own way but doesn't send the message that we're putting in an effort for ourselves or our partners. We don't mean you need to have a full face and stilettos or a full suit and tie on every day, but every now and then it can go a long way to just take a little extra time on your appearance, break out of the pajama bottoms, and try something a little more seductive.

4. Take a trip down memory lane with your partner. Thinking about happy times or special memories can elevate levels of serotonin in the brain. Try watching videos or looking at photographs of your early months or early years together. Try reenacting those moments—for example, if one of your first dates was a hike to the top of a mountain followed by Mexican food and margaritas, do that hike together and follow it up with a visit to the same Mexican restaurant.

5. Try new activities together. When you are trying something new, like learning a new language or doing a pottery class or archery or beer making, you're creating new brain cells—new neural pathways—and activating pleasure centers of the brain that release dopamine. And you're giving the two of you opportunities to spend more time together. Take turns trying an activity your partner wants to try—even if you're not sure either of you will enjoy it. You'll still connect, and if it is a disaster, you'll have a funny memory to look back on.

Celeste and D'Andra: Mild Relationship Symptoms Related to Boredom

Self-described homebodies Celeste and D'Andra rarely go out for dinner, they both like nothing better than a good book, and most of their holidays are divided between each other's aged parents, siblings, or adult children. At fifty-six, Celeste is stepmother to D'Andra's children from a previous marriage, who both live two thousand miles away and work at a large tech company. D'Andra had Jason and Jemma in her early twenties but was a single parent when she met Celeste at age thirty. Their blended family and their life together have been a happy experience for most of these years, but Celeste has started to feel restless; a bit of "is this all there is?" has entered her mind. And D'Andra has noticed that her partner of twenty-one years has stopped kissing her hello or crawling on the couch and cuddling with her unless D'Andra specifically asks Celeste to join her.

Celeste and D'Andra are displeased not so much with each other as with their daily lives. D'Andra is actually pretty pleased with their patterns, saying, "I love the life we created. . . . There's nothing I enjoy more than reading next to each other on the couch at the end of the day or having our coffee in the morning listening to the birds." However, as happy as D'Andra is with their life, she is not pleased with having an unhappy partner—and Celeste is not happy. Celeste is watching time go by and she wants more excitement, more new things or activities, and more places to help her feel alive. She puts it this way: "I feel older, and I don't want to. I don't think time is endless anymore, and I want to use some of it differently. We've raised our kids, and we've been good parents—but I really want more 'me' time and more 'us' time. I think D'Andra is happy enough, but I'm not. I need to pull her out of the life we've lived and have her see how much I need a change. . . . If I didn't say anything, we'd go to the same restaurants and same vacations for the rest of our lives. I need her to see that I can't do that anymore."

Phil and Georgia: Moderate Relationship Symptoms Related to Boredom

Phil and Georgia are looking like they might be on the road to separation. When they were living together, their lives were one adventurous activity after another. Double-black-diamond skiing and scuba trips to Belize and other exotic destinations were things they did together and a major reason why they got married. But children changed all that. While Phil still loved adventure, Georgia began to love loafing. The two boys just sapped her of her energy. Still, she hated leaving them, so she wouldn't. Pretty soon, Phil was doing all the adventures by himself, with friends, with couples, with anyone who would go with him. Now, six years into the marriage with two kids under five, he feels uncomfortable just sitting at home but is lonely on vacation. He has recently suggested marriage counseling to Georgia.

Phil and Georgia need more intervention. Phil has started to create a parallel life for himself, and eventually he won't be able to remember why he is married to Georgia. Couples generally become fragile if they decide that the best way to get what they want out of life is to go their own way and allow the marriage to become a shell, a space without adequate input, emotion, or fun. If they give up on refueling the marriage, they are courting its demise. Part of this issue can be filed under "I am not going to compromise or let this person diminish my chances of enjoying what I like, so I am going to just go out and do my own thing."

This is essentially what Phil is doing—without taking responsibility for helping the marriage fail. He says, "Our schedules just don't work out. I used to sit around waiting for us to sync, but I was missing what I wanted to do. So after some years of waiting around for her, I decided to take charge of my own life. I have buddies I ski with—not something she does at my level—and I have sports I do myself that she finds boring. Then I spare her my family, so I visit them alone. So I know it looks bad, but there's good reasons why this happened. Not that big of a problem, but I admit sometimes I wish I had a wife with me. . . . OK, sometimes I am lonely."

Some separate vacations do not necessarily undermine a marriage—but if most of the leisure-and-fun time is taken away from the marriage, how much is left to sustain it? Marriage is a collection of experiences, memories, problem-solving, and conversations. Two people have to share enough to feel connected and invested. The couple thinks they have more or less solved their issues by living parallel lives, but now that a parallel pattern has been established, it is hard to bring the couple back to each other. This kind of marriage has been labeled "devitalized" by some researchers—which is to say, the couple is stable but inert. There is little time together, few exciting moments to share, and a depletion of positive experiences. It may last until death do they part, but with a loss of joy. Or one or both partners get entranced by someone they do share a life with (a coworker, mutual sports enthusiast, etc.) and a vulnerable marriage falls apart.

Samantha and Carl: Severe Relationship Symptoms Related to Boredom

It seems clear to Samantha that Carl doesn't like her company anymore. He doesn't want to go try new restaurants (which he used to do). In fact, he often picks up carryout for dinner on the way home from work and generally eats alone. During the time of COVID-19, he would hole up in his home office and not take breaks to talk to her. Samantha said, "He acts like I don't exist." They still take vacations, but only the ones that he has always taken with couples they've known for years. He has rebuffed her ideas about new places she'd like to try. When they are with old friends, he spends more time with them than her; Samantha believes that he is avoiding being alone with her. Worse, he makes fun of her in front of the other couples quite often, talking about her almost in third person, such as "Oh, no, Samantha would never want a charter boat. She'd have to cook!" She feels stifled and unloved. Carl feels like

Samantha checked out of their marriage a long time ago, saying, "She stopped wanting to do things with me and every time we would go away alone, we'd just end up fighting the whole time. . . . She would never dress up just to go out with me. She stopped acting like our marriage mattered—the only time she ever tries to look nice, it's because we're meeting up with her friends."

Samantha and Carl are reduced to bouncing back and forth between non-stop bickering and a cold war. They may have lost the possibility of being able to have fun together because the underlying goodwill and connection that used to be in the relationship seem to be missing. Once contempt (discussed in chapter 7) enters the picture and friends are used to undermine a partner's status in the group, things are dire indeed. Instead of taking on their issues, whatever they are, Carl takes potshots and Samantha endures them but then takes the opportunity to get in some licks of her own. They have evolved into tolerating each other—but sometimes barely doing that. They still do some activities together but hide behind friends because doing so helps them have a life. When asked about their marriage, Carl either clams up or offers derogatory statements about his wife ("She's too lazy to join us" or "My wife can't pull off a swimsuit like your wife, so she's not going to join our trip") or the marriage itself ("Isn't marriage inevitably boring?" or joking with an edge, "Aren't most serial killers husbands?"). This couple has to get back common courtesy, respect, and a better connection before fun of any kind will be experienced as enjoyable.

RELATIONSHIP Rx FOR EACH COUPLE

Couple: Celeste and D'Andra

Prescription: Relationship Vitamins: Couples Bucket List Now and Then, How and When; Date Night Out of the House

Celeste and D'Andra were a couple who used to have fun and were still emotionally connected. One of them was reasonably content with the life they had, but they were badly in need of some renewed delight and bonding experiences. We know many of you can relate, so if this is you, here are a few things you could do—all in service of getting rid of the "is this all there is?" blues. And while some bouts of the relationship blues are necessary (as they say, "Into each life a little rain must fall"), others are avoidable or fixable with a little bit of imagination and the determination to re-create moments of wonder and excitement.

Couples Bucket List Now and Then, How and When

Celeste and D'Andra would benefit from trying an activity we like to call a Couples Bucket List Now and Then, How and When. The exercise goes like this: Each partner can work, on their own or sitting in the same room together, on writing all the things they have always wanted to do either on their own or as a couple. They can ask themselves or each other, "When I die, what do I want to make sure I've done, tried, experienced, or seen?" and "What have I always wanted to do that I still have yet to try?" These answers can vary widely—they could include places to travel to, hosting a Mardi Gras party (or going to Mardi Gras!), getting a couples massage, learning to knit, going zip-lining, trying axe throwing, taking a tantra class, learning astronomy, or trying a new language. On their lists, they can make three sections: one for short-term or more immediate items they could do relatively easily (scheduling a couples massage), one for things that may take a little bit of planning and coordination (learning to knit or hosting a party), and one for the big-ticket items that will take significant planning to pull off (going on a trip to Paris or hiking in Patagonia). They can then combine their lists to make one big bucket list. After they have their combined list, they can talk through the how and when of each item. For example, learning to knit may involve finding a knitting class, buying supplies, and deciding when to fit this activity into their days or schedules together. A trip to Patagonia may not be doable for a few years, but they could talk about finding a travel agent, researching the trip and where they must go, buying hiking gear, and putting money aside to pay for the excursion. Making a couples bucket list together can be fun—there are inevitably going to be some negotiations as you each try to prioritize what you want to try first. There will be a few rights to refuse on some (e.g., skydiving), but with limited exceptions (even if it's not your cup of tea), we suggest couples go all in, even if reluctant.

Celeste and D'Andra completed this activity and identified that D'Andra had wanted to take Latin dance classes, which was exciting to Celeste. Inspired by this idea, Celeste immediately found a class nearby and they enrolled for a session to start the next month. They both had listed Paris and Provence on their long-term lists, which was funny to them, as they didn't remember talking with each other about it. Celeste had on her list that she had always wanted to learn how to cook French food, so they started frequenting a small authentic French restaurant not too far from where the dance studio was and befriended the chef there, who explained his recipes and each week would give Celeste a recipe to try. Inspired by Celeste's new love of French cooking, they planned a two-week trip to France for the following year, which of course included a cooking class they could do together. This very easy exercise was exactly what this couple needed.

Date Night Out of the House

By now, you know that we are fans of date night. For those who are homebodies, it is critical that you find opportunities to get out of your comfort zone (which we know is your couch for many of you!). Doing so stimulates new areas of the brain, gives you opportunities for new shared experiences, and can radically fight off the boredom blues. But you have to leave the house. The other rule of thumb is to make sure at least half of your activities are physical—this allows for rushes of adrenaline, which improves the mood and can sometimes influence sexual desire. Celeste and D'Andra were coached to participate in an alternate date night (described in chapter 4) that had to involve being out of the house, couldn't involve visiting family members or doing what would ordinarily get them out, and had to be something new and different to them. Celeste and D'Andra took their bucket list and focused on the first section; many of those activities—things they hadn't done before—could be made into a date night, whether they were trying ice skating, trying Ethiopian food, going fishing, or seeing an opera.

Couple: Phil and Georgia

Prescription: Relationship Medicine: "The Way We Were" Exercise; Bucket List; Marriage Enrichment Classes

Georgia and Phil were living under the same roof but had been living different lives. Boredom set in for each of them, and instead of coming together, they began to develop their own lives, routines, and even travel plans, separate from each other. At this rate, their marriage was in jeopardy of divorce, infidelity, or another major catastrophe, something that neither of them wanted. When faced with boredom that has led to this dynamic of parallel lives, it can be helpful if couples can be reminded of their early years together—as a way to draw them back to each other.

"The Way We Were"

Each of you is charged with finding at least twenty photographs or videos of your early months or years together. Then find a time to sit down together (make it fun, so pop the popcorn, break out the cheese plate, and pour some tea or rosé). You'll want to set aside one to two hours for this activity. Take turns sharing each photo or video and talking about what that event or experience together meant to you. As you're sharing, see whether there are any of these experiences you might want to re-create!

Phil and Georgia loved this activity. Sharing some of their early photos had them both laughing and crying—sometimes both at the same time. Georgia surprised Phil with a video of their first hike together, and they decided to start hiking again on the weekends, beginning with returning to the place they took the video (so many years ago!) and making a new video.

Bucket List: Play the Supporting Cast and Create New Opportunities for Connection

Parallel existences in a marriage must be modified—you didn't sign up to be married to live separate lives, nor did you sign up to be unhappy. Addressing parallel existences will require both partners doing things outside of their comfort zones. Georgia and Phil had neatly divided their lives into nonoverlapping events, but they could feel the coolness between them increasing over the passing months—and they really didn't want to go into so deep a freeze that they couldn't defrost. Given the stakes, this couple, like all couples in this situation, had to make a promise to each other that they would either learn each other's obsessions (golf, skiing, keno, etc.) or go on these outings and learn how to support their partner in the process. For example, if skiing is important but you can't or don't want to ski, be there to do breakfast, meet at the lodge at lunchtime, and prepare hot cider and hors d'oeuvres at the hotel rental or ski condo for the gang. But just supporting your partner's interests won't do it all; new mutual interests also have to be developed that will encourage respect, admiration, fun, and conversation.

Here are some ideas:

Volunteer together. Doing good work together enlarges the heart. Seeing each other show compassion and liking yourself better because of what you are doing can go a long way personally and in your relationship. It could be volunteering at the humane society, cleaning up a local park or beach, fixing a house with Habitat for Humanity, or cooking for a day at a women's shelter. It could be going big and helping Doctors Without Borders for weeks or a month or even traveling to another part of the country or world to help a community after a disaster. Volunteering is good for you; doing it together is good for the relationship.

Take lessons together. As we have said before, doing something new together is a tonic for the relationship. Take a Spanish class in anticipation of going to Mexico. Learn carpentry or welding and build something together. Georgia and Phil completed the same Bucket List activity as Celeste and D'Andra. Georgia decided she would learn scuba diving so she could go to Belize with Phil, and while she didn't love it like he did, she liked it enough to go in the mornings but not go on the second dive in the afternoon. When Phil went in the afternoon, she would stay back to read and get drinks and snacks ready for when he was done for the day. They both also took massage lessons, which went a long way toward easing their post-scuba muscles and, more important, reigniting their sexual life together.

Marriage Enrichment Classes

When the boredom and lack of communication have resulted in the two of you getting so distant that interaction is awkward, it's important to recognize the problem and get some skilled help in learning how to relate again. Enrichment classes are not group therapy, but they have some elements that help couples recognize their mistakes and learn new ways to engage and understand each other. Enrichment weekends also often include fun things to do, like hikes or resort activities. Some of these can be expensive, so couples who are tight on cash may want to look into programs offered by their churches or other organizations.

Couple: Samantha and Carl

Prescription: Relationship CPR: Couples Therapy; No More PDA (Public Displays of Arguing)

When contempt is present (as described in chapter 7), couples are in serious need of an intervention. Without being overdramatic, we believe that contempt is like cancer: it builds and spreads unless a major intervention occurs. Contempt is particularly bad when one or both spouses are so angry that they use the presence of other friends, couples, or events to take shots at each other. Of course, no one likes to be around that, so people will either avoid being with the couple or further exacerbate the situation by wanting to be with only one of them without the other. Decreases in social connection aren't good for you as individuals or as a couple.

In the case of Samantha and Carl, something has so soured this marriage that the first thing to do is to go to couples therapy to staunch the microaggressions that appear in both public and private. Underneath those remarks are true anger, fear, and/or disappointment, and unearthing what is going on has to be done as soon as possible. Forget date night. This couple can't have fun or enjoy each other if they are too angry or too alienated to see the possibilities left in their relationship. A talented therapist can help them get out of a cycle in which each spouse feels punished. If one or both partners are making this task difficult or impossible, individual therapy might be required as well. But while it is hard to believe, when a couple is at their nastiest, there often still is a road back.

In the case of Samantha and Carl, it turned out that much of the anger present in the relationship was the residue from a failed joint business investment that forced them to downsize their lifestyle. Samantha could not stop talking about losing the house she loved, and Carl felt emasculated, demeaned, and disrespected, which came out sideways in the nasty comments he made about his wife. In therapy, in the midst of the pandemic, they came to understand how much they needed each other—and, in fact, that if they stopped punishing each other, they could actually enjoy the time they had together. After several months, they were feeling motivated to get back to the relationship they had and started making their own couples bucket list and prioritizing each other. They learned to stop airing their dirty laundry to others—and even apologized to their friends for putting them in that position, explaining that they were at a low point in their relationship but committed to making it work in a way with which they were both happy. It is amazing sometimes how deep a chasm a couple can climb out of if there is motivation to do so.

Summary

Boredom, while part of life, does not have to be the reason we end relationships or even fantasize about being with other people. Relationships with routines and predictability are also relationships that are secure, dependable, and comfortable. Even couples who have been together for decades can maintain relationships that have periods of excitement, adventure, and newness, but both partners have to be willing to identify when boredom might be cropping up and put the work in to create new opportunities for adventure, fun, and connection.

7

DISRESPECT AND CONTEMPT

My partner disrespects me. I feel humiliated. He is so selfish. I can't believe I let someone treat me this way for so long. Is this relationship abusive? She thinks she is so much better than me. I would never do this to her! How did we get here?

Nobody gets married or embarks on a long-term commitment and says, "I'm going to be the biggest @#$% I can be to my partner," or at the altar vows, "I'm going to become someone my partner grows to hate," or thinks, "I will put up with as much negativity as one could possibly tolerate in a relationship." Yet many couples will, over time, end up in a place where they don't recognize the person in front of them—or even the person in the mirror—and ask themselves and each other, "How did we get here?"

So many marital or relationship disputes come down to problematic communication. In his groundbreaking book *What Predicts Divorce?*, renowned relationship researcher Dr. John Gottman identifies the most problematic types of communication in couples and models the four warning signs of a failing marriage after the four horsemen of the apocalypse: criticism, contempt, defensiveness, and stonewalling.[1]

Criticism

Criticism is attacking our partners' characters or their core beings and is different from voicing a complaint (e.g., "I was upset when I didn't hear from you today" versus "You are so selfish to not even think of calling me!"). The partner who is criticized ends up feeling attacked, rejected, and hurt. Over time, couples may end up in an escalating pattern in which criticism increases over time and becomes more intense, eventually leading to worse horsemen like contempt.

Contempt

Contempt is a complete lack of respect for our partners (e.g., name-calling, eye-rolling, using constant sarcasm, or ridiculing them). The partner on the receiving end of contempt feels unworthy and unloved. The partner who is showing contempt toward their partner acts as if he or she is morally superior to the other. More on contempt later.

Defensiveness

Defensiveness typically is a response to criticism—when we feel attacked, we respond in a way to protect ourselves. When relationships are struggling, there tends to be a higher rate of criticism and thus a higher degree of defensiveness. When we feel blamed or accused of something, we search for excuses and play the victim so our partners will back off. We reverse blame in an attempt to make it the other partner's fault. Although a common response to feeling criticized, defensiveness is rarely successful at resolving conflict. By deflecting blame or coming up with excuses, we end up dismissing our partners' concerns and send the message that we don't take our partners seriously and that we won't take responsibility or accountability for our mistakes. Ultimately, defensiveness really is a way of blaming our partners, and it does not allow for healthy conflict management or resolution.

Stonewalling

Stonewalling is the final horseman and usually occurs after one partner feels so overwhelmed by the poor or toxic communication, including contempt, that he or she needs to escape the dynamic. This partner's systems become flooded, and he or she ends up shutting down and withdrawing from the other partner. Rather than working to resolve the conflict or engage the other partner, he or she may ignore the other partner, give the other partner the cold shoulder, zone out, physically turn away, or act busy and engage in other activities. When we are engaged in stonewalling, our downstairs brains take over (i.e., that attachment system we talk about in chapter 2), and it becomes harder to utilize the areas of our brains responsible for problem-solving and rational thought.

Disrespectful treatment falls on a continuum from sarcasm, repetitive criticism, eye-rolling, or ignoring to more extreme versions such as contempt, which is characterized by overt hostility, humiliation, and disgust toward a partner in which one person asserts moral or intellectual superiority over the other. Disrespectful treatment is at the very least annoying and at its worst insufferable and abusive.

Sometimes we suffer in ignorance—we simply don't know that our behavior is disrespectful because, for many of us, it's just a way of life. Perhaps you grew up with people like parents or siblings who provoked you, took aim at your flaws (or what they perceived as your flaws), and regularly slammed or joked you into submission until they had the upper hand. Perhaps a form of rebellion (or self-defense) developed, like a pattern of retorts that you developed as part of a repertoire of defensive jabs so you were able to give as many hurtful comments as you received. Sure, some of these potshots at one another were seen as more or less well meaning or described as banter, included in the coziness and permissions of family. But maybe other times, or perhaps consistently, the verbal arrows hit their targets, and whatever your responses appeared to be (funny or sharp, or just remaining quiet), the truth was that you were not impervious, and those arrows pierced your self-confidence and even your vision of your own lovability. There are many of us who grew up in homes where disrespectful words or behaviors were just part of the family culture—we may have watched our parents treat each other with contempt in which one parent always seemed to have the upper hand or superiority over the other parent, who was viewed as defective in some way. These patterns could be insidious and hard to identify, or they could be more overt displays of horrible name-calling and abusive behavior. When this is the only home that you know, this is your "comfort zone," and it can be hard to shift that relational template without significant work on your part.

Experiences like these—in families, friendships, sports leagues, fraternities, or elsewhere—made some of us tougher, and some of us weaker, but few of us happier. Even worse, these experiences may have set the stage to use these micro- to macro-aggressions as the common language in even our most treasured relationships. In romantic relationships, it may start off as playful banter or repartee—a ping-pong game of back-and-forth snarkiness. Over time, what may have started as innocent banter or criticism meant to "help" the other can evolve into deeper wounds. Partners may say that comments were not meant to hurt the other, but the swipes at each other are often masking deeper feelings—such as anger, rejection, or other types of personal pain—that result in us inflicting control or pain on the other. When these shots become common, they constitute a daily program of assault as they batter their receiver. Paradoxically, they also batter their deliverer because the person who goes after his or her partner is full of unresolved anger and other feelings he or she may not yet be able to identify—unresolved pain that is corrosive. So, while not excusing this behavior, it is important to note that whether a person is being disrespectful or is the victim of disrespectful remarks, each person is struggling—and the relationship is suffering as well.

Let's look at various levels of disrespect and contempt and some ways to address them.

Couple #1: Perry and Jenny: Mild Relationship Symptoms Related to Disrespect and Contempt

Perry and Jenny have been together for just over a year. They enjoy each other's company and their "banter" between one another. Lately, however, Jenny is experiencing Perry as "sensitive," while Perry complains that Jenny is being "overly critical of me," and this issue is hurting their relationship.

Couple #2: Prisha and Arjun: Moderate Relationship Symptoms Related to Disrespect and Contempt

Prisha and Arjun have been married for eight years, and while a couple of years were, in their opinion, pretty good, they both are unhappy now. Prisha feels that Arjun is constantly criticizing or demeaning her; Arjun believes he is trying to make his wife "better" and argues, "Isn't it my job to help her become a better person?" Prisha feels like nothing is good enough for her husband, and she has begun to avoid him and dread their time together.

Couple #3: Mack and Pamilla: Severe Relationship Symptoms Related to Disrespect and Contempt

Mack and Pamilla have been together for twenty-five years, married for twenty-three of these years. The conflict between them has grown so much that their relationship is marked by constant trading of barbs, including behavior that one could argue is verbally abusive. Mack has turned to public humiliation and flirting as ammunition against Pamilla; Pamilla is under significant pressure from her friends and family to leave Mack.

All three couples are struggling with instances (or long patterns) of disrespect, and for our second and third couples, contempt has crept into (or is overtaking) their relationships. All three are in need of some tools and strategies to improve the positive communication between them and either prevent disrespectful treatment from worsening or stop contempt in its tracks before their marriages are devastated.

Sure, we're all going to have moments in our relationships when we say things we don't mean, lose our cool under stress, or say hurtful comments we can't take back. How bad can disrespect get? We think the danger zone begins when one or both partners actually become contemptuous. Moderate disrespect might manifest as continually interrupting one's partner, but it bleeds into contempt when the message, either verbalized by the interrupter or felt by the one being interrupted, is that the interruption is not an overeager desire to talk, but rather a statement that the partner has nothing really interesting, important, or relevant to say. That the partner's opinion doesn't matter. That the partner doesn't matter. It could be as gross as a spouse saying, "Oh, don't listen to him. He's not worth listening to. He couldn't tell a story right to save his life." Some forms of contempt are harder for people to identify—they believe they are being genuine or "just telling the truth." They take the higher moral ground with statements like "I'd never do that to you" or "How would you like it if I did that?" Often, this person is more of the lecturer, talking to his or her partner as if the partner were a child. Other times, he or she might mock or make fun of the partner. When contempt enters the scene, one partner is asserting that he or she is smarter, has better morals, or just is a better human being than the other, while the other partner feels worthless, flawed, or ashamed. It's no surprise that contempt is the number-one predictor of permanent separation or divorce.[2]

When this kind of treatment becomes more than rare—and when it is either unrecognized or unapologetically delivered with intent—any relationship, much less a marriage, is in big trouble. Whether intentionally or not, the whole idea of partners having each other's backs is betrayed. Instead of "it's you and me against the problem," our partners are now the opponents. We never know when we might be attacked or undermined—and the problem is never solved. Contempt sometimes stems from individuals feeling that they are standing up for themselves—which is usually a healthy thing to do—but the problem is that they are standing up for themselves against their partners, trying to raise themselves up while tearing their partners down. So unless the conduct is recognized and the underlying issues resolved, the relationship, instead of being a safe refuge from the world, is now a war zone—and what a sad thing that is.

Contempt isn't just bad for our marriages—it's also bad for our health. Research has shown that individuals who use contempt in their communication have higher rates of disease, including cancer, heart disease, and other illnesses such as colds or the flu.[3] We need one another to survive. Contempt cuts off or threatens those ties to other people, including our most precious relationships. Thus, it's no surprise that, biologically, contempt is bad for our own physical and emotional health and well-being.

So let's say you have identified some degree of contempt in your marriage—it does not mean you immediately need to call a divorce lawyer. For couples who are committed to fixing their relationships, there is hope and there are concrete solutions that can be applied to get them out of this toxic pattern. In relationships, we don't have to get it right all the time—and there is much value in the repair.[4]

Contempt is often seen in individuals who grew up without an expansive emotional vocabulary. If feelings were represented by colors, they'd have the tiny crayon box you get at restaurants with the primary colors—they are able to acknowledge only mad (angry, pissed off, etc.), happy, and perhaps sad feelings. Those who have that coveted extra-sized crayon box of feelings are able to identify and express more difficult-to-name feelings: shame, rejection, irritability, fear, betrayal, jealousy, insecurity, and so many others. That is why the remedies for contempt will inevitably include increasing feelings vocabulary and opportunities to express true feelings in a safe way.

Mr. Fred Rogers said it best: Anything that is human is mentionable. Anything that is mentionable is manageable. Often, what leads to contempt are feelings we have had that have not yet been named. We can make painful feelings, which are universal to all human beings, mentionable by giving them names and increasing our emotional vocabulary and by creating a safety zone in our relationships to express these feelings. Once we make the unspeakable speakable, we are able to figure out a plan to manage those feelings in a way that is healthier, more productive, and respectful.

In addition to increasing feelings vocabularies, another powerful remedy to contempt is to give genuine appreciation to our partners. You've heard how important expressing gratitude can be (#blessed), but it's not just a cliché. To reverse the damage of contempt and prevent it from happening in the first place, we want to increase connection, do some repairs, and create a culture of appreciation within our relationships.[5] In this way, we're able to notice more of our partners' positive qualities rather than the negative ones. Ideally, we want our positive statements and gestures to greatly outweigh the negative ones—the magic ratio is at least five positive statements or feelings to one negative one.

How might you remedy contemptuous communication? Here's a strategy:

1. State what you're feeling.
2. Add a request.
3. Invite your partner to the conversation.

For example, instead of saying, "I can't believe you accepted an invite to your parents this weekend instead of our date night! You're such a selfish jerk. You never think about my feelings or anyone else's!" you might say, "I feel disappointed and annoyed that you decided to accept the invite without talking to me first. I feel sad, as I was looking forward to spending some time together" (stating feelings). "I'd like to avoid this happening in the future by you coming to me first" (adding a request), "and I'd like to talk with you about how we can do that" (inviting your partner to talk about it). Other ways to invite your partner into the conversation include statements like "What do you think?" or "I'm curious to get your thoughts" or "Is it OK for us to talk about this?" Here are some more examples of contemptuous comments and corrected approaches that remedy the contempt.

Situation: One spouse makes lunch and doesn't make the partner anything.

- Contemptuous comment: "Seriously? That's a @#$%&# move. You're so selfish—you made lunch and didn't make me anything?"
- Remedied approach: "I felt left out seeing you make lunch, and it makes me feel good when you make me something too. I miss sitting down together during the day and connecting with you. Do you think we could have lunch together tomorrow? Can we talk about this?"

Situation: One partner shows up late for the child's basketball game.

- Contemptuous comment: "You showed up so late for his game again! What the @#$% is wrong with you? You're always so late—I would never do that to our kids. What kind of father are you?"
- Remedied approach: "I felt anxious and annoyed that you couldn't make it on time to Jonny's game. It's important to me for our kids to see that we are supporting them together and that you are on time. Do you think we can talk about a plan that might work for you so you're able to get there on time?"

Situation: One spouse brings up the same old fight, again.

- Contemptuous comment: "You're bringing up a fight about something that happened four years ago? You need to get over it—it's getting insane. You're crazy. You need some serious help."
- Remedied approach: "Hon, I feel confused and frustrated and think there's a missing puzzle piece here. I want to make sure that we can resolve this together so it doesn't keep coming up. Would you be willing to talk this through with me so we can figure out how to help you move past it?"

Let's do a closer examination of our couples.

Perry and Jenny: Mild Relationship Symptoms Related to Disrespect and Contempt

Although they have not been in their relationship for all that long, Perry and Jenny both see each other as their long-term partner. However, lately Jenny believes Perry is paranoid because if she makes any kind of joke about him—about what he's wearing or some experience he had—she feels that he's way oversensitive and reactive. Perry, however, doesn't think it's funny to make fun of his unruly hair, his preference for sandals with socks, or his reluctance to be the life of the party like she is. He feels she lectures him way too often, treats him like he is a child, and makes him think that she doesn't think he is understanding her or other people when he is tracking them just fine. He feels that while she is generally a kind person who means well, in his case, she is too critical and too superior and she *is* going for him, and he wants to stop it.

Jenny thinks that she is just giving Perry advice, but she has made him feel like she doesn't respect his ability to make good decisions or even give him the right to dress the way he'd like. Jenny explains that she grew up in an Asian American home where it was part of her family culture for her loving parents to be particularly hard on her and her siblings, and criticism was part of daily life. She acknowledges that she had some anxiety because of this issue but for the most part believed that her family was trying to make her better, which is what she believes she is trying to do with Perry. Perry says that he realizes that he is not an "underwear-model kind of guy," but he never was, and she fell in love with him just the way he was. He gets particularly ticked off when she overexplains things to him, treating him, he feels, like an inept boy. "I know," he says, "what 'mansplaining' is, but I get 'womansplaining' and I don't think it's any better when a woman does it. Jenny thinks she's kidding around, but you know, you can only take so many snarky comments on your shoes, or not dressing appropriately, or not getting the 'real' message of a movie, before you feel like you are being dissed. . . . I love her most of the time, and I really want this relationship to work, but I don't even like her when it feels like she's trying to make me feel small. And to be honest, I don't care if she's trying to put me down or not—the effect is the same, and I don't seem to be able to get her to cut it out."

If Jenny isn't careful, she may be unintentionally damaging her relationship by making Perry feel unsupported and disrespected. She says, "I am just trying to make him better. He has such a beautiful body; he could wear such lovely clothes and look so good. I think just a little tweaking here and there would make all the difference. But he really resists and fights me on it when it's such a little thing."

Here's the rub: It is not a little thing if he doesn't think it's a little thing. And it is generally a bad idea to fall in love with people and then want to do complete makeovers of them—whether it's their clothes and appearances or their interests, friendships, or other relationships. Yes, people can change in ways that are positive (see chapter 1). Yet people fall in love, and stay in love, because they are adored, respected, and understood for who they are. While Perry and Jenny may have started out that way, Jenny's behaviors are eroding what began as a mutual attraction and acceptance of each other as is.

Prisha and Arjun: Moderate Relationship Symptoms Related to Disrespect and Contempt

Prisha and Arjun have been struggling regarding Arjun's increasingly disrespectful treatment of his wife. Arjun is frequently critical of Prisha, mocking her or rolling his eyes when she tries to talk about anything other than household issues or their young children, and has made light of her attempts to write poetry. He treats many of her ideas (even simple ones on where they might spend the holidays) as ridiculous and often is sarcastic about her work. She works in a preschool, and he makes fun of her low salary and what he considers overinvolvement in the lives of the children she works with. He makes her feel like nothing she does is right. Prisha, dreading their dinners together at the end of the day, has been numbing her anxiety with more wine than she should have in the evenings or going to bed early with their youngest child and often complains of headaches. Arjun explains that he has been frustrated that Prisha doesn't seem to be "content with being a mother. . . . I thought when she had children, she'd focus more on the children and creating our home together. . . . Instead, she wants to talk about anything but our family!" Prisha feels controlled by Arjun's treatment of her—she feels as if she is disappointing him as a wife and a mother. She explains, "He acts as if I can't have my own interests or my own ideas separate from his or our family's! No matter what I say or do, it's never good enough or smart enough for him." She feels that he exerts power and control over her as it pertains to their finances: "I know I make less money than he does, but I also care for our kids and this home, and that should count for something. He thinks he's better than me because he has a bigger paycheck—and he is sure to let me know it." She confesses, "I wish I could escape sometimes. Lately, the only thing that gives me any relief is wine—and I know I'm drinking more than I should—or when he goes away for work!"

In thinking about the four horsemen, Prisha and Arjun have unfortunately experienced all four. Here's an example of a recent fight and what criticism, contempt, defensiveness, and stonewalling look like in their marriage: Arjun returned home late from work, while Prisha worked in the morning and returned home in the afternoon. Arjun had been so busy he did not get the chance to let Prisha know he would be home late until he was ready to leave the office. When Arjun finally returned home, he was exhausted, but so was Prisha, as she had been working, followed by working from home while trying to care for their kids, who were cranky and ready for bed.

Criticism

Prisha: "Arjun! You are so selfish. You are always putting yourself before me. You always just think about yourself, never about other people or the impact of your actions on others."

Arjun: "Seriously, Prisha? You don't appreciate how hard I worked today. You are just looking for a fight when you should have been getting the kids in bed and cleaning up the house, which, by the way, is a total disaster."

Contempt

Prisha: "You are the absolute worst. I'm here all day working and taking care of the kids, and you come home and sit your lazy ass on the couch with your phone while I have done literally everything around this house."

Arjun: "You are pathetic. What the @#$% is wrong with you? You can't even take care of yourself, let alone these kids. I ran meetings all day, and you haven't even changed your clothes since yesterday. You look like an unattractive mess. And what kind of mother lets their kids run around in this mess? A terrible one. I can't believe I married this."

Defensiveness

Prisha: "I didn't clean up the house because I was too busy actually being a family and doing all of the things with the kids you should be doing with them too, like their homework and packing their lunches."

Arjun: "I didn't come home on time because I was late to work cleaning up the house you left a mess last night. By the way, why would I want to come home to this? If you could get things done and the house in order, maybe I'd actually want to come home sooner."

Stonewalling

Arjun turns on his video games and stops talking to Prisha. Prisha gets up and busies herself with the dishes, refusing to acknowledge Arjun when he walks in and out of the room.

Mack and Pamilla: Severe Relationship Symptoms Related to Disrespect and Contempt

Mack was a doting husband for at least the first fifteen years of marriage. But he turned on his wife as they entered middle age. He became angry about a lot of things—the government, his treatment at his job, the economy—but he takes his frustrations out most cruelly on Pamilla. She has become afraid to have friends over or to go out to a dinner party because that is when he is at his worst. Mack will talk about her "sweating like a pig" at night or make comments such as how she went to law school but was too dumb to pass the bar and now has to settle for "crappy" jobs at the courthouse. To make matters worse, he fawns publicly over pretty women at his office. Recently, when he was all over women at a dinner party, Pamilla said that he was embarrassing her, to which he replied, "You are the embarrassment. . . . You are the reason I need other women." She broke out crying at the time, and, instead of seeing that his wife was in pain, all he could say was how she embarrassed him at the event. Mack will demean her to her face both behind closed doors and with others watching. One reason their once-active social life has diminished is because Pamilla's friends and family have said they do not want her to stay with her husband and they do not want to watch how he treats her.

As we mentioned earlier, if disrespect or contempt has entered your relationship, you are not alone. If this is the case with you, you feel disrespected or nagged. Or if you are accused of being disrespectful or nagging, there are several exercises you can do to get out of this bad habit of disrespecting your partner's style or opinions.

RELATIONSHIP Rx FOR EACH COUPLE

Couple: Perry and Jenny

Prescription: Relationship Vitamins: Off-Limits; Code Word; Use the Magic Ratio

Off-Limits

Start with three categories: nagging, jokes that aren't so funny, and hurtful words. Each partner is challenged with writing down an example or recent event in each category. Nagging could include your partner constantly reminding you to pick up after yourself. Jokes could include examples of when your partner is joking, but it hurts your feelings or rubs you the wrong way. Hurtful words could be times when you felt very upset, offended, or criticized by your partner. When starting this exercise, enter it with two core assumptions: that the intention is not to hurt the other or make the other feel stressed out or upset, and that the feelings the other has (even if you didn't intend to hurt them) are valid.

After creating your lists, you will then share them by reading them to each other. After saying what bothered you, state how it made you feel and what you need from your partner. Your partner will have the opportunity to repair this prior communication by apologizing, acknowledging your feelings, and making a plan for the future.

For example, Perry said, "I feel disrespected when you make fun of my clothes. I know you don't mean to hurt my feelings, but it does. You may not realize how often you make fun of what I am wearing, and I am sure you don't want me to feel bad, but I do." Then Jenny could apologize and say that she didn't want him to feel disrespected: "I'm really sorry that I made you feel disrespected. That wasn't my intention. I love you just the way you are. Sometimes I bring it up if we're going to an event together and I'm worried you might be underdressed." She could then ask him, "If I'm worried you may be too underdressed for an event, is there a way I could say that to you so it wouldn't feel like an insult? Or will any comments or suggestions about your clothing feel too insulting to you?" In either case, she could find a new way to ask him to dress differently, or she could know that any clothing suggestions would be violating a boundary of his and she could stop it altogether. The point here is to talk about real feelings, stop behavior that feels disrespectful to a partner, and, if possible, see whether there is another avenue for change that is not disrespectful and certainly not contemptuous.

Code Word

Given that Jenny grew up in a home in which criticism was part of being a loving family member, it might be hard for her to identify or contain it initially. Therefore, it might be helpful for them to come up with a code word they could use if Perry was starting to feel criticized, such as "cactus" or "slippery slope" or whatever cute term they wanted to use.

Use the Magic Ratio

Perry and Jenny could also make sure to work toward the magic ratio of five to one—for every negative feeling or statement they might need to express to each other, they would need to make five positive statements or gestures. Although it sounds simple, we encourage couples to try to track their communication patterns over a week or two to notice just how often they may be engaging in negative interactions (e.g., nagging, criticizing, ignoring, eye-rolling) versus positive ones (e.g., praising, complimenting, doing something nice for the other partner).

Couple: Prisha and Arjun

Prescription: Relationship Medicine: Expand the Crayon Box and Practice Using Those Crayons; Twenty Things I Love about You; Individual Therapy for Arjun

Some people are so critical that it destroys their partners' feelings of acceptance and being loved for who they are. That was what was happening every day to Prisha when Arjun found something else to criticize. To be fair, this was how Arjun grew up. His father criticized his mother, and his mother, in turn, criticized her children. It was hard for anyone in that family to be good enough. Criticism was as ordinary as having breakfast—but not even close to being nutritious. In fact, everyone in his family was starving—for praise and acceptance. Arjun was also told that he had to be superior to everyone else, so part of the way he reinforced that feeling was to look for ways he was better than his friends, his wife, and even his kids. But since this way of acting was so well known to him, he didn't think about the damage it was doing until Prisha summarily moved out to her mother's place in the same neighborhood, taking their young children with her. He did not want a divorce and was embarrassed that she would let her family know that she was unhappy. But this action did motivate him to understand why she was so angry and unhappy—and to do something about it.

As described above, contempt often stems from a lack of emotional vocabulary to express how one is truly feeling. Although this may be a challenging task for Arjun (and others who grew up in homes in which feelings other than anger were not readily expressed), it would serve him well in the long run. The assignment is to intentionally express a feeling five times per day—each must be a different feeling, and they must not all be in the same category (e.g., anger, pissed off, irritation, and rage). You can find a reference for over 270 feelings words in chapter 3. There are also feelings color wheels, feelings emojis, and other resources online with various ways to depict lists of feelings. Ideally, Arjun would be able to intentionally express his own feelings. But if he found that task difficult at first, he could start with characters in books, pop culture, or television. This may seem silly and awkward—like learning a foreign language—but the idea was that over time, feelings language would become more comfortable and he would be less likely to use strategies like contempt to mask what was beneath. Further,

Arjun and Prisha could utilize reflective listening as opportunities for him to express his feelings in a healthier way—and for him to also have the opportunity to truly listen to his wife and develop a better understanding of her position and her feelings.

Twenty Things I Love about You

One exercise to counteract our feelings that our spouses see us as worthless is to go on an appreciation campaign—creating that appreciation culture we talked about earlier. This can be done in front of a therapist, but it also can easily be done at home. The task is for each of you to draw up a list of twenty things you love about your partner. Write those things down on a piece of paper and then say them to one another. If that sounds daunting, it shouldn't be. There are hundreds of things to love about a partner, even if there are also things that are annoying or worth changing. But if the whole operating mode of a relationship has been contemptuous, then the marriage needs a huge counterweight so each partner can come back to feeling loved and respected. After this exercise, you and your partner can challenge yourselves with adding to this list over time—and making sure you're sharing it with each other.

Individual Therapy for Arjun

Of course, this wasn't the whole answer. Given the impact of his statements on Prisha and the origins from his childhood, Arjun needed to do some work on himself in individual therapy to find out why he needed to belittle his wife and how to stop this behavior, immediately. He needed to realize how many things she did well, rather than just giving the compliments as a way to pacify her. If he couldn't do this deeper work, the marriage would ultimately fail or be a cold-war zone. But a good beginning was a genuine apology, a true show of appreciation, and a number of reassurances to his wife that he could respect her. If he was able to do this work, not only would Prisha feel loved and accepted, but we also guaranteed that Arjun would experience a sense of relief and freedom with learning that he did not have to be superior and that imperfection in all of us is a beautiful thing.

Couple: Mack and Pamilla

Prescription: Relationship CPR: Breaking the Fourth Wall; Individual and Couples Therapy and Consultation with an Expert in Domestic Violence

In television, there is a concept known as *breaking the fourth wall*. It's a strategy wherein the actor (or the reality television expert) turns to the audience and disrupts the fantasy that everything the audience is watching is real by talking directly to the audience, explaining what was really happening behind the scenes. That can feel intimate, or it can feel like a betrayal, since you have to acknowledge that the television star or actor is admitting that you, an audience member, are now in on the fact that this is a television show and not necessarily real life in real time—and you must join the fantasy as a character now, which is something you may not be able to do.

Why do we bring this idea up? Because there are some fantasies that we know are not real, but we don't want to be confronted with an absolute end to them—and there are times when, as relationship experts, we have to break the fourth wall with couples to let them know how bad things really are. Pamilla had been deluding herself that she was still in a marriage, but what her husband did betrayed everything a marriage is supposed to be. He demeaned her, but, even worse than that, he demeaned her publicly and in front of friends—this behavior was nothing short of abusive, and Pamilla needed to understand that *she was in an abusive marriage*. She had endured this treatment for a long time, and it had emboldened Mack to become more fearlessly nasty and cruel. It is more or less the death of our marriages when our spouses become our constant opponents. While Mack's contempt was certainly not good for him and his own health, it had destroyed his wife.

To be clear, based on all that had happened behind the scenes, as much as we believe people can change and we believe in the power of therapeutic intervention, we weren't sure that Relationship CPR could save this marriage. It was on its last gasp, and it needed oxygen badly. And it was emotionally dangerous and abusive. (For more on abusive relationships, please refer to the National Domestic Violence Hotline at https://www.thehotline.org.) Since the behavior was habitual, Pamilla needed to go to a therapist, with or without her husband. We strongly suggested that she work with an individual therapist skilled in helping survivors of emotional and verbal abuse who could also talk through safety planning should she choose to leave the marriage. We want to be clear that just because Mack had not been physically abusive to Pamilla, it doesn't mean this was not an example of domestic violence or intimate partner violence—in fact, psychological maltreatment (name-calling, public humiliation, shaming) can be just as damaging or even more damaging than physical abuse. Mack needed to agree to work with a therapist skilled in anger management who had expertise with domestic violence. If Pamilla decided that she wanted to save the marriage, Mack also would have to go to a couples therapist with her, and he would have to know that if he didn't attend individual and couples therapy, the marriage would end. Surprisingly, it often takes this final declaration to save a marriage, even when you think the offending partner is beyond change. Mack may have had the experience in which he realized that the result he had been creating was not actually the result he wanted. In this case, he had been taking out his anger by waging his war against the world on his wife and had gotten used to abusing her. But there were other consequences—children's reactions, economic consequences, and his own continued unhappiness—that he may not really have wanted. So this last gasp would either have the happy outcome of finally getting Pamilla out of a disastrous situation or help her husband understand how awful his behavior was and how much change was required for him to have a wife who wanted to stay with him. In any case, both Mack and Pamilla had much work to do.

Summary

There are going to be times when we all behave badly in relationships. Some disrespect will happen, but when that lack of respect rises to the level of contempt, relationships are in serious trouble. Remember that most of the time, the repair matters as much as the love that you have. You aren't going to get it right all the time, but if you and your partner can learn from each other what hurts, what is off-limits, and how you each can best feel respected, supported, and loved, you both can have a safe refuge in each other from the rest of the world and avoid a cold war or an all-out war zone in your marriage or relationship.

8

HOUSEHOLD
RESPONSIBILITIES

*How does he not see the dishes piling up? She doesn't appreciate everything I
do around this house! I feel like I literally do everything for this family. I'm
exhausted—I work all day, and then I come home and I work all night.*

Although talking about the dishes isn't something you would consider
doing in the early phases of dating, couples might actually stave off
a lot of arguments and tension if talking about household responsibilities
were prioritized. Dishes aren't sexy. Lawn care isn't romantic. Laundry has
nothing to do with lust. Yet division of labor—dividing up what needs to be
done—if done right, can pave the way for smooth sailing. As we talk about
in chapter 5, our expectations often are what interfere with our happiness.
Household responsibilities can be a source of high stress—yet it's not the
responsibilities themselves, but rather the ambiguity regarding who is doing
what and how things are divided. This ambiguity leads to resentment, tension, and someone ultimately having a freak-out over the dishes or who did
or didn't call the cable guy.

Research on marriage has shown that among the things that lead to
contentment in a relationship, household responsibilities rank third after
faithfulness (commitment) and good sex.[1] Sharing chores is important to
relationship success. Despite so much progress in the last fifty years regarding gender equity, household division of labor is still highly influenced

by gender.[2] Research has also shown that gay couples actually perform the best when it comes to navigating household responsibilities. Same-sex couples tend to communicate better, share chore duties more fairly, and assign tasks based on personal preference rather than gender, income, hours worked, or a power position in the relationship.[3] However, recent research has found that when gay and lesbian couples have children, they often begin to divide things as heterosexual couples do.[4] One partner takes on a greater share of household chores and childcare, while the other partner focuses on making more money.

Let's take a look at three couples.

Couple #1: Laura and Lizette: Mild Relationship Symptoms Related to Household Responsibilities

Our first couple, Laura and Lizette, have been together for five years but have lived together for three. They recently have been arguing more about priorities—Lizette believes they need to spend more time "being adults" and getting things done at home, whereas Laura wants to be carefree and spontaneous.

Couple #2: Beatriz and Marco: Moderate Relationship Symptoms Related to Household Responsibilities

Our second couple, Beatriz and Marco, have been together for thirteen years with a strong marriage and love for each other. Even though they both have demanding jobs, Beatriz has been carrying the majority of the household responsibilities and parenting due to the fact that Marco is often traveling. Beatriz is extremely stressed out—and Marco is clueless as to what to do, which just upsets Beatriz even more.

Couple #3: Camille and Davis: Severe Relationship Symptoms Related to Household Responsibilities

Camille and Davis have been married over fifteen years. Early in their relationship, they fell into traditional roles. Camille thought this situation would change as their relationship matured, while Davis was satisfied with his wife doing the bulk of the "women's work" around the home. Davis had extremely high expectations that his wife maintain a clean home with dinner on the table every night. Their communication broke down years ago, and, notably depressed and anxious, Camille vacillates between trying to please her husband (she now says she fears his tantrums) and staying in her bed doing nothing for hours.

All three of these couples have in common conflict over division of labor in their homes and relationships, ranging from mild to severe symptoms. All three of these couples could have benefited from conversations earlier in their relationships regarding expectations about sharing the load and what that might look like. One thing they don't tell you when you're falling in love is that it feels amazing to swing from the chandelier, but somebody still has to change the light bulbs or call the electrician when it breaks. And we know that nobody likes to be a nag or to be nagged; yet all three of these couples are set up for what is called the "demander-withdrawer pattern."

As two career-driven women who are also mothers, we would love to be able to tell you that gender equity has been achieved when it comes to dividing the workload. Sorry, my dears, we can't tell you that. There is a well-documented disparity of the division of labor in the household. Women tend to take on more of the household responsibilities—even if they are working equal or longer hours and earning higher salaries. On average, women tend to perform twice the number of tasks and assume more of the mental labor or cognitive load (planning and coordination of tasks). Additionally, when studies compare leisure activities to household activities, men have the highest degree of leisure activities and time spent on leisure while women have the least. So the research tells us that women are not only working more and doing more but also having less fun!

Ladies, we know that it is no surprise to you that women still carry the largest household workload and the largest cognitive and emotional load. It's BS, but it's true. "Cognitive load" refers not to the actual task itself but to all the thinking and planning that is task related. For example, going to the grocery store involves making a list of what you need, checking the fridge and pantry to see what you're running low on, and talking with family members (spouse and/or kids) about what they might need. "Emotional load" refers to the worry and strong feelings associated with tasks needing to be done and taking care of yourself and others. Having children adds to the cognitive and emotional load tenfold (see chapter 11). Not surprisingly, given the higher cognitive and emotional load, research has found that heterosexual women are the least satisfied when it comes to division of labor being fair.[5]

We aren't here to tell you that the responsibilities have to be divided fifty-fifty—that's just not practical or realistic. But, as boring and tedious of a conversation it might be, *clearly outlining the expectations related to household responsibilities* (circa chapter 5) is a relationship lifesaver. Not having household responsibilities outlined—not communicating about all that is expected—leaves room for one person to feel he or she is doing the lion's share of the work, resulting in conflict.

Navigating household responsibilities is more than just talking about your to-do lists. Although the division of labor between men and women is well documented, studies have found that the nuanced ways couples interact with each other about and during these tasks are linked to relationship satisfaction and overall well-being.[6] Household tasks are a good barometer of communication and represent a complex set of interpersonal exchanges that enable couples to achieve solidarity and closeness—and feel like they are on the same team. Couples who struggle the most lack clarity on *the what, the when, and the how* of household responsibilities being carried out.

If you haven't established clear roles, routines, and expectations yet, you are not alone. The majority of couples haven't. Yet it's worthwhile to have those conversations and engage in exercises that facilitate the communication about the laundry and the lawn mowing. Couples who have a clear and respectful understanding of each other's roles and tasks don't spend as much time negotiating responsibilities, and life flows more smoothly for them. Keep in mind that what works for one couple might not work for another, and it is up to you to decide what that division of labor looks like. Dr. Jessica worked with a couple who decided to have a clear line between inside chores and outside chores in which the husband did all the chores indoors (laundry, cleaning, etc.) while the wife, who grew up on a farm, did all the outdoor chores. That worked for them. There are also couples who decide to share the majority of tasks—by doing them together—which allows for more time to connect and a feeling that they are partners, whether it's paying the bills or carrying in firewood. That strategy might work for you, or it might not be practical. It's up to you and your partner to come up with a plan that makes sense.

Having a mutually shared understanding minimizes the need to nag the other partner or judge his or her work. Nobody likes to be nagged, and nobody likes to be labeled a nag. When you're clear about who is doing what, when, and how, you eliminate the need for nudging or engaging in what is often called the "demand-withdrawal pattern."[7] The demand-withdrawal pattern refers to one partner (typically but not always a woman) believing that the other partner is engaging less in accomplishing multiple tasks and family-related tasks, while the other partner (typically but not always a man) complains about being constantly nagged. In this pattern, one partner (the demander) nags, complains, or makes a demand of the other partner, while the other partner (the withdrawer) avoids confrontation, withdraws, and becomes defensive. Withdrawal responses can take many forms: avoiding intimacy, avoiding conflict, or even giving angry responses. This is similar to behaving like one of Gottman's four horsemen: criticism, contempt, defensiveness, and stonewalling (which we mention in chapter 7). The demand-withdrawal pattern is a reliable indicator of maladaptive communication and can even predict future relationship distress!

In coming up with a clear spoken plan, you will eliminate the all-too-common situation of one partner feeling that the other partner "doesn't know how much I do around here" and takes him or her for granted. Conflict is much more prevalent when couples haven't worked out dividing responsibilities in the home and need to negotiate and renegotiate division of labor from one day to the next. The more ambiguous the expectations are, the more conflict there is. The more conflict there is, the greater the chances are for engaging in power struggles, expressing dissatisfaction, or even using controlling behavior.

Based on our work with couples and the science backing up communication about household responsibilities, here are five "don'ts" when it comes to navigating who is doing what at home:

1. *Don't expect that household chores should be fifty-fifty.*
   It turns out that relationship satisfaction isn't dependent on it being a fifty-fifty arrangement, but rather on how close the arrangement is to each partner's ideal division of labor. It's the perception of fair division that matters, not the division itself.

2. *Don't expect that you should do only what you're good at.*
   Avoid falling into the trap that just because you're good at cooking means you're the one who should do it. Anyone can learn to chop vegetables! Sometimes trying something outside of your comfort zone is good for you, and it's good for your partner to see you making an effort.

3. *Don't avoid speaking up and don't ask for help.*
   A lot of couples therapists will tell you to ask for help when it comes to household responsibilities. We aren't those therapists. In addition to not speaking up about things feeling unfair, a huge mistake you can make in your wish to have your partner do more chores around the house is to ask for help. Asking for help implies that the responsibility for the chores belongs to just you, when, in the real world, household responsibilities fall on both partners, so it's up to both of you to figure out a solution.

4. *Don't consistently do your partner's agreed-upon responsibilities.*
   This one is easy. If you do it for them, they don't learn how to do it, they don't get the credit for pulling their weight, and you end up resentful and exhausted. So stop doing that.

5. *Don't underestimate how much sharing the responsibilities can lead to more sex!*
   We'll let you in on a dirty little secret: couples who share more housework have more sex. There is something satisfying (in more ways than one, wink wink) about sharing the workload. Research has shown that couples who share the housework have more sex and greater sexual satisfaction and are happiest when they divide tasks the most evenly, especially taking care of the kids—a pressing concern for many parents (more on that subject in chapter 11).[8] In relationships in which both partners clean the bathroom, these couples have sex nearly two more times each month than when women shoulder the responsibility alone. Forget about lingerie, date nights, or romantic weekends away—the couples likely to be having the best time in bed are those who are doing the laundry together or at least rotating the responsibility every other week. And if not sharing the housework together, when couples

perceive that the division is fair, they are happier in their relationships, have sex more frequently, and are more satisfied with their sex lives.

"But with all that needs to be done, there's no time left for us." Don't let that thought get in your way! Look at chores as opportunities for more time—more time with each other, which also means cutting down time doing chores. Chores can become a joint effort for married couples, cutting cleaning time by two-thirds and even helping enhance physical attraction and leading to a better sex life.[9]

What household responsibility leads to the most sex? Dishes. It's not just about an equitable division of labor; the *types* of chores men and women share make a difference in their marital happiness. Typically, men want to share the shopping, and women want to share the dishwashing. For women, dishwashing is huge. Women who found themselves doing the majority of dishwashing reported significantly more relationship conflict, lower relationship satisfaction, and decreased sexual satisfaction than women who shared the dishwashing with their partners.[10] Interestingly, research has found that men who share household shopping with their partners report greater sexual and relationship satisfaction than both men who do most of the shopping and men whose partners usually do the shopping. This result suggests that people are not necessarily made happier by allowing their partners to do all the work but are most content when tasks are shared.[11] Interestingly, husbands who embark on grocery store runs with their wives report greater sexual and relationship satisfaction than those who have to make all the trips to BJ's or Whole Foods on their own. Before you get all "duh, no one wants to stand in line at Walmart by themselves" on us, here's another surprising finding: It's not even about passing the task off to someone else. Chore sharers report greater satisfaction than those who rely primarily on their partners to keep the kitchen stocked. But, as with any relationship between two people, the division of labor that comes with a household and kids is complicated and needs to be personalized for that couple. If one of you prefers to fold a towel a certain way, perhaps you should be the one to get the clean clothes from the dryer. At the end of the day, how you divide household responsibilities is personal to *your* relationship and up to you to decide, together.

Talking about household responsibilities is likely to get a little messy. There will probably be some sort of tension or unpleasantries when navigating household responsibilities. Interestingly, conflict over household responsibilities highlights poor communication patterns or is a symptom of a larger issue. So how do you have these conversations? What can buffer the tension? Here are a few suggestions:

- Approach the topic in a lighthearted way, and don't be afraid to use humor to neutralize the tension.
- Use "I feel" statements: "I feel overwhelmed by the demands of the laundry; I need you to work with me to figure out a plan." "I feel anxious looking at the pile of clothes; maybe we could fold the clothes together."
- Use the reflective listening technique we mention in chapter 2 to work through any disagreements about the division of labor.
- Set aside time to have a "business meeting" about the topic, free of distractions and armed with worksheets or a notebook to help you literally be on the same page.

Laura and Lizette: Mild Relationship Symptoms Related to Household Responsibilities

Our first couple, Laura and Lizette, are madly in love. Lizette manages an art gallery; Laura is a painter who also works as a bartender. They met at a work event Lizette was hosting. They had a commitment ceremony to each other two years ago. Lately, they keep butting heads around differences in how they should prioritize their time. Laura says, "We're still young; we should be going out more!" Lizette believes that they need to start being "more responsible and getting more done around the house and planning for our future" when they aren't working.

Lizette has become increasingly annoyed with Laura, feeling like Laura "needs to grow up" and "it's time to start adulting." Laura, anxious about how their relationship might change if they stop doing the things they always did (e.g., going to clubs, having late nights out with friends, and sleeping in on Sundays and having long mimosa-soaked brunches), puts a lot of pressure on Lizette to "have more fun." Laura works a couple nights per week at a nearby bar and grill and likes to stay late after work and have Lizette meet her. While this routine was fun for a little while, Lizette grew impatient with all that needed to be done in their home. They had a huge fight after their electricity and heat were shut off—not because they couldn't afford it but because Laura forgot to pay the bill—and this happened on more than one occasion. They love spending time with each other and are both reasonably happy with their intimate life, but when they are together, Lizette often is distracted by all the tasks that need to get accomplished, while Laura is annoyed by Lizette's distracted behavior and says that she feels like a "child who has a list of chores from Mommy and that's not sexy." Lizette, often resentful, either does many of the tasks that need to be done, such as grocery shopping, or feels like she's constantly nagging Laura to do "basic things most people should just know to do!"

Beatriz and Marco: Moderate Relationship Symptoms Related to Household Responsibilities

Our second couple, Beatriz and Marco, have a solid marriage—yet they continue to have the same arguments in which Beatriz feels like she carries the lion's share of the workload. Beatriz works full time as a tax attorney, while Marco works in sales for a technology company, which requires a busy travel schedule. Beatriz has been caring for their home and their kids and trying to manage her full-time job, but she is exhausted, stressed, and unhappy. She feels like she's a single mom and says, "I don't feel like I'm part of a team." Marco sees how stressed Beatriz is and wants to ease her burdens, but he has no idea what to do. When they see each other, they either fight or are both too exhausted to argue. They still have an active sex life when they see each other, but Beatriz says, "It's like the same robot sex every time," and to her "it's just one more chore on the list." Beatriz has been having more physical complaints, such as more frequent colds, headaches, and difficulty sleeping. She's feeling depressed, has more wine than she probably should at the end of the evening, and is up at three o'clock most nights worrying. It has become very clear to her and those around her that the workload has taken a toll on her physical and mental health—which, if not handled, could have severe consequences. Marco, who deeply loves his wife, is also exhausted from his travel schedule and, when he's home, can see that Beatriz isn't happy. He does what he can to try to take the load off on the weekends, but he feels like it's not enough and that he has to play catchup when he gets home from trips as to what he's missed and what needs to be done. He also feels guilty being away from his kids, so he likes to spend as much time as he can having fun with them—often relegating the discipline and homework to Beatriz.

Camille and Davis: Severe Relationship Symptoms Related to Household Responsibilities

Davis, a state trooper, prides himself on always having a clean home and coming home to a warm meal on the table. Camille works part time at a hair salon. Early in their marriage, they fell into more traditional roles in which Camille was happy to cook and clean and Davis handled the yard work on the weekends. They had two children, and Camille carried the vast majority of child-rearing responsibilities but got increasingly resentful of Davis, who would criticize her parenting and was always "the fun dad" while she had to be the disciplinarian. Davis was highly demanding of Camille, to the point that if he came home and dinner wasn't on the table, he would either yell at her or give her the silent treatment. Camille became highly anxious over time, dreading when Davis would come home from work.

Camille says that she walks on eggshells and has a pit in her stomach before Davis comes home from work, saying that she will scan the house to make sure that it's clean, and even if she's exhausted from her day, she will skip a catnap or doing something nice for herself just to make sure that dinner is in the oven before he gets home. She originally "loved taking care of him," but now, she says, "I'm just Davis's wife, and most times I just feel like my job is to make him happy and do what he wants me to do, and I do it because it avoids a fight or him acting like an ass." She's fantasized about starting a business of her own, having a hair salon out of their home, but is afraid to even mention this idea to Davis, as it would upset their family dynamic. She feels bitter and most days can't stand the sight of him—lately, she's been staying in bed longer than usual and just recently has stopped doing much of the housework, telling Davis that she's not feeling well. Davis, who is rigid in a number of ways when it comes to his exercise routine, his daily schedule, and his expectations, has gotten increasingly aggravated with Camille. If she fails to "perform" or meet his standards of what he expects to be done around the house and do what he says is "women's work," he belittles her, calling her lazy or comparing her to his friends' wives. Davis approaches his wife with a sense of entitlement (e.g., "She should do this for me because she's my wife and that's what a good wife does")—a quality that does not bode well for a healthy marriage. Sadly, although they established an unspoken pattern early on in their relationship, they never openly communicated about their ideal expectations for what their roles might be.

RELATIONSHIP Rx FOR EACH COUPLE

Couple: Laura and Lizette

Prescription: Relationship Vitamins: Household Responsibilities Task List; Practicing Acceptance

Lizette and Laura had very different ideas about what constituted cleanliness. Lizette frequently referred to herself as the "house manager" and felt like she was taking on all the emotional and cognitive load of trying to run the household, even though they were both working full time. She would notice things needed to be done before Laura did and said, "I always have to tell Laura what should be done." Lizette did the bulk of the shopping because she felt like she'd just have to fix what Laura bought—like the wrong kind of dishwasher soap or the wrong cheese for lasagna—and by doing it on her own, she avoided a bunch of texts from the store from Laura. Lizette and Laura would benefit from taking full stock of their household responsibilities, learning about one another's priorities, and then discussing who is responsible for what and along what timeline.

Household Responsibilities Task List: What, When, How, and Who

There are countless lists for household responsibilities available online that can help you with this exercise. Using a list of your choosing or generating a list on your own, each of you can make a list of all the possible household responsibilities that apply to your relationship and household situation. Each couple's list will be different. Here are some examples of what might be on your lists:

- Making beds
- Vacuuming the home

- Cleaning bathrooms
- Doing laundry—cleaning, folding, sewing, ironing
- Cooking
- Shopping
- Doing the dishes
- Removing snow
- Cleaning up the pool or deck
- Taking trash out and to the curb
- Doing maintenance on the house—minor repairs, cleaning out gutters, cleaning the garage
- Caring for the lawn—mowing, raking, weeding, gardening
- Taking care of the cars—maintenance, washing, getting gas
- Paying bills
- Tracking finances
- Buying gifts or cards for loved ones
- Organizing help or hiring contractors
- Doing tasks related to childcare
- Keeping track of the family calendar

After you each have your own list, compare the two lists and then combine them. With the combined list, each of you ranks from −10 to +10 how much you enjoy versus despise each responsibility.

After reviewing all the possible household responsibilities that applied to their home and relationship, Laura and Lizette talked about their priorities when it came to their home. Many couples, like Laura and Lizette, find that they look at the division of chores differently. For example, a messy house or clutter doesn't bother some people. However, if you are comfortable with a messy home, but it bothers your spouse, you *both* need to compromise. Compromise works best if you select priorities rather than try to completely satisfy both partners. As unsexy as it sounds, discussing your own and each other's feelings about unmade beds, manicured lawns, bills being paid on time, and clutter around the house can help you figure out what to prioritize. For example, if you feel that the kitchen should be clean at the end of the evening, you need to share that information with your partner so you both can have a better understanding of what's important to each other. Laura and Lizette discussed how Lizette felt more at ease when the home was clean and there was a plan to pay their bills on time. They worked together to set all their bills to auto-pay so Lizette didn't have to worry and Laura was off the hook for remembering. Laura discussed how she wanted to be able to contribute but also that she wanted to spend more time with Lizette rather than feel like when they were home, they were "still working."

They eventually negotiated a plan that made sense—they talked about all the different household responsibility domains and determined what they each would do versus share. In reviewing their household responsibilities list, they worked to anticipate roadblocks. Each of them highlighted the chores they absolutely despised doing. They were able to negotiate that if one of them didn't mind that chore, that person would do that chore; if they both detested the chore, they would either take turns completing the chore or do it together and then celebrate completing it (e.g., over a mimosa-soaked brunch, much to Laura's delight). In order to address Laura's concern about not spending as much time together, they decided to include more joint shopping. This approach allowed Lizette to feel like Laura was invested in helping get things done around their home and planning for meals during the week, and it allowed the two of them to have more time together. They agreed to at first have a weekly business meeting to talk about what was coming up in the week (meetings, errands, special occasions, etc.), review their plan, and make a list they posted on the fridge that they both could refer to. A couple months later, both described having more harmony over household responsibilities and how it played into their day-to-day satisfaction. They had regular conversations every couple months to recalibrate things and make sure the plan was working.

Practicing Acceptance

Lizette and Laura could also benefit from a simple strategy of practicing acceptance. There are going to be characteristics or behaviors our partners demonstrate that irk us. That's just part of being human. We can prevent a lot of headaches if we are able to accept perceived flaws and embrace these as quirks or just part of the package. For example, one of us has a partner who has a habit of leaving his coffee mug on the table instead of putting it in the dishwasher. This used to drive one of us crazy, complaining, "Does he not see the mug? Who does he think is going to clean up this mug? Does he think I'm his maid?" Until one day, one of us decided that we were going to accept this behavior and that, in marrying him, we agreed to pick up his coffee mug every morning and we're OK with that. That might be a deal breaker for some of you, but for one of us, it was a no-brainer—once we looked at it as part of the package, it became an ongoing joke and we no longer had any resentment with that coffee mug (or its owner). Laura had a habit of leaving her clothes on the bathroom floor rather than putting them in the hamper in the bedroom. This drove Lizette batty until she decided to accept it as part of Laura's free-spirited charm and either pick up the clothes or move another hamper into the bathroom.

Couple: Beatriz and Marco

Prescription: Relationship Medicine: Household Responsibilities Task List and Technology to the Rescue; Consider Outsourcing; Weekly Business Meeting

Based on Beatriz's characterization of their sex life as "robot sex," Beatriz and Marco could definitely benefit from some of the exercises in our sex-and-attraction chapter (chapter 4). But beyond that, there were a number of exercises—and frankly just conversations—that could really help them when it came to household responsibilities.

Household Responsibilities Task List and Technology to the Rescue

When one partner travels, it is inevitable that responsibilities will fall more largely on the partner who is home. That does not mean that the partner who is away can't also contribute significantly to what needs to get done. Beatriz and Marco reviewed their household responsibilities lists and how they ranked their chores. Marco said to Beatriz, "No wonder you're exhausted!" They laughed together and began to unpack their list with the task of determining what Marco could pick up from afar, using technology to his advantage, and what might be worth outsourcing. We talk a lot about how technology can sometimes interfere with relationships, but when there is distance because one spouse is traveling, technology actually can work to your advantage!

Marco talked about his guilt related to traveling and the kids; Beatriz said that she understood but constantly felt like she had to play teacher and disciplinarian all the time. They came up with a plan for Marco to review the kids' homework in the evening—he set up a half-hour Zoom call with each child. This plan took the pressure off Beatriz, who would do yoga or take a bath or do some other relaxing activity during homework hour. They also downloaded a shared calendar app in which they were able to list tasks that needed to be done. Marco agreed that if work was needed related to the home (such as calling the electrician or setting up the dog-grooming appointments), he would try to get these calls done when his workload was light. They used a shared app for grocery and discount-store shopping so they both could add items to the cart as they thought of them and agreed to have groceries delivered whenever possible.

Consider Outsourcing

You and your partner can review your household responsibilities, and if your budget can handle it, consider outsourcing some tasks. For example, if one of you can't or doesn't want to lower your standards when it comes to household cleanliness, you can hire some outside help, budget permitting. This should not be viewed as help for one partner (Beatriz, for example) but as help for both partners.

Although Beatriz always took pride in maintaining a clean home, she and Marco decided together to outsource cleaning to a cleaning company twice per month. In convincing Beatriz, Marco said, "I chose the job that makes me travel because it pays me more . . . but it takes me away from you, so at least I can help ease our burdens and have more time together as a family when I'm home." Beatriz, who reluctantly complied with Marco's idea, found the cleaning service so helpful that they quickly changed it to a weekly cleaning. Now, Marco jokes that "eighty bucks a week has saved our marriage." Beatriz agrees.

Weekly Business Meeting

Marco and Beatriz agreed to have a weekly business meeting to talk about what was coming up—if Marco was traveling, they did it over FaceTime or Zoom, no matter what. This is an example of a couple for whom it did not make sense to assume that the division would be fifty-fifty—the bulk of the load fell on Beatriz. But remember, it's *when the load is unspoken* that problems emerge. It is the perception of fairness that matters and having both the support and the appreciation of our partners to manage that load. In their business meetings, Marco would check in with Beatriz; he would ask, "What do you need?" and "How can I help support you this week?" This made all the difference. If something Marco had agreed to do hadn't gotten done, instead of nagging him about that, Beatriz had their business meeting to check in on that task. The resentment Beatriz had toward Marco melted, as she felt like even though she was still managing a larger share of the responsibilities, he was fully invested. She had a better understanding of his needs and concerns, and he had a better understanding of hers.

Couple: Camille and Davis

Prescription: Relationship CPR: Couples and Individual Therapy

Camille and Davis were in hot water, and, if you ask us, Davis's treatment of his wife was unacceptable and bordered on abusive. If we were Camille's girlfriends, we'd be giving her the number of a good divorce attorney. But as professionals, we also know and have seen ourselves that with the right help, change (even related to deep-seated issues) is totally possible. We suggested working with a couples therapist and perhaps individual therapists for each of them. In therapy, the couples therapist could work with Camille and Davis regarding effective communication about expectations and lay out ground rules for what was no longer acceptable (e.g., name-calling, stonewalling). In individual therapy, Camille could address her low self-worth, symptoms of depression, and why she had tolerated this treatment from Davis for so long; Davis could work on what appeared to be some deep-rooted misogyny, expecting that his wife's job—and her identity—were to please him and that there's "women's work" and "men's work." Over time, if they were able to commit to saving the marriage and had made gains in sticking to the ground rules, the couples therapist could consider working through a household-responsibilities list and encourage role play in which each of them engaged in completing the other's tasks and responsibilities for at least a week.

Summary

The research is very clear—there are disparities when it comes to household responsibilities. Yet couples who share responsibilities are happier and closer and have longer-lasting, more satisfying relationships with better sex lives. When the dishes are getting done, the sheets are getting steamier. When it comes to division of labor, we have learned that couples who have laid out a clear plan and have communicated this plan are the most successful. The conversations might be boring or messy, but they are worth the effort. Armed with the right tools, when they make the unspoken responsibilities spoken (and even written out), couples literally can be on the same page, which allows both partners to feel valued and respected and that both are contributing to their family.

9

MONEY AND FINANCES

Why does she spend so much money on shoes? I feel like we're financially drowning, and he doesn't seem to notice. I'm always the one in charge of our finances—my partner doesn't even know how to look at our account balance. I want to retire young; she seems to just want a bigger house.

You probably have heard that money is one of the most treacherous topics in marriage. You have not heard wrong. Money is one of the foundational elements of survival—in whatever form that society uses to get essentials (shelter, food, health) and luxuries (vacations, prestige cars, private schools, etc.). When you put together couples and money, you're bound to get some conflict. Did you know money is the number-one issue married couples fight about?[1] When it comes to marital problems, conflict over money is the second-leading cause of divorce, behind infidelity. Studies have shown that 70 percent of couples argue over money—more than over chores, sex, or children![2]

The key to preventing financial fights? Talking about finances. More than 50 percent of people in "great" marriages talk about money daily or weekly, while only 29 percent in "OK or in-crisis" marriages do. Ninety-four percent of people in "great" marriages discuss money dreams together; 45 percent in "OK or in-crisis" marriages do.[3]

Yet talking about money isn't easy. We are socialized not to talk about money or financial concerns; some research has estimated that more than 90 percent of people avoid talking about money. On top of that, when we do talk about it, we aren't always honest—one in three of us have lied to our partners about our spending.

If there is too little money, we worry about meeting daily needs, and we may blame each other for not earning enough or for managing money badly or for having bad judgment. Conversely, while having a lot of money is better than having too little, it may influence our personalities (i.e., we get too impressed with ourselves), and it certainly doesn't guarantee a happy marriage (think about the divorces of Bill Gates and Jeff Bezos, famous billionaires who were married to very impressive women).

Issues about money can be like termites, in that the proliferation of small creatures can weaken the very structure of a house if not attended to, or like the proverbial elephant in the room, a crushing weight that is impossible to ignore. And yet it is one of the least-talked-about subjects when people fall in love—at least in modern Western countries. In some other parts of the world, like India, arranged marriages investigate the economics of the bride- or groom-to-be, the family's financial status, and their overall caste and class. If the economics or education or a number of other factors are not to their liking, either or both families will probably decide not to make the match. In most Western countries, we salute love and say that it is the most important thing about a couple's future—but, in truth, we do take in economic information. People who marry tend to have similar educations and economic potentials, and that's not an accident. We care about money; we just care about love as well—and sometimes love (and sexual attraction) allows us to overlook the fact that the people we are in love with may not make the kind of money we expect to live on, may not share our values about what to spend on and what to save, and may not feel comfortable with our own economic styles or habits.

Thus, we have couples in conflict on this topic—a lot. So here are our three couples in various levels of distress.

Couple #1: Leticia and Kai: Mild Relationship Symptoms Related to Money and Finances

Leticia and Kai have very different money habits and values. Leticia comes from an immigrant family that is now comfortably middle class, but she experienced soul-crushing poverty as a small child. Her parents worked very long hours and had to take low-paying jobs when they first came to America in order to provide a "better life" for Leticia and her siblings. As a result, even though she has created a thriving small business, Leticia is very scared of not having enough money again. Kai grew up more comfortably (financially) than Leticia. His parents owned a small but successful electronics store that he worked in as an adolescent. He saved money from those years, and with his savings and parents' help, he was able to go to college with no debt and the confidence that he could make a good living. Occasionally, he likes to "live large and spend large," which scares Leticia.

Couple #2: Lars and Peter: Moderate Relationship Symptoms Related to Money and Finances

Lars and Peter have several conflicts over money. Much of this disagreement relates to Lars's frustration with Peter's use of their mutual credit card. Peter likes to shop—and he means it when he says he does "retail therapy." And lately, he's needed a little more therapy than usual. As a result, the card is almost always overdrawn, and since they can't pay it off every month, extra fees have been levied. Lars, thrifty and careful about all money matters, is extremely upset about Peter's disregard for their budget and the amount of time Peter spends online buying stuff.

Couple #3: Margo and Jack: Severe Relationship Symptoms Related to Money and Finances

Margo and Jack have been together eight years and married for six, and this is a second marriage for both of them. They have just had a major blowup since Margo found out that Jack has been hiding his gambling addiction for a very long time and also has credit cards that Margo didn't know about, each of which carries serious debt. Margo is both scared and angry since they are a married couple and one person's debt affects both of them—she is terrified that they will not be able to have the life she envisioned for them when they retire and will not be able to support their children in the way they both had dreamed.

Our couples have all discovered that money can create significant stress in their relationships. Each of these couples could benefit from open communication about their values and their finances—learning how to be more comfortable being "financially naked" with each other. If they are able to improve their communication about money and their lifestyles, chances are that they could increase the harmony and even have better, more comfortable futures with each other. However, they first have to learn how to talk about their finances.

We must be aware of our own comfort levels in discussing finances—some of us are much more comfortable than others. Some of us might be finance nerds (like Dr. Jessica's husband) and are used to talking about money every day. For others, we weren't socialized to discuss money or finances, and it feels awkward. There are also those of us for whom finances are a hot-button issue, one that we associate with power, control, or status.

If we are newer in our relationships, we may not need to become "financially naked" with our partners or we may be less comfortable doing so—that's OK. It's up to each of us and our partners to decide when we are ready to tackle these issues. But if we're already married, plan on being in long-term committed relationships, or are getting ready to tie the knot, now is probably the time to start having these conversations.

Further, many adults have intensive risk aversion and intractable fears (which often stem from childhood trauma) around money, scarcity, and risk, and these fears make discussing even the slightest changes in profession or career very overwhelming. The key is to approach the discussion not as a fight or a negotiation but as an open, calm, respectful discussion about how both partners envision their family life together—what they want, what they don't want, what's important to them, and what their top priorities are. It helps to state those things as calmly as possible and understand that all of this is deeply personal and individualized. No one is "right" or "wrong" in what he or she feels.

Everyone's personalities are different, and opposites tend to attract. Chances are, in your relationship, one of you loves working with numbers (the nerd) and the other one would rather not be tied down by what the numbers show (the free spirit). One of you might be the saver, while the other is more inclined to spend. While those differences can cause some marital problems, *they aren't the real issue.* The source of the problem is whenever one of you neglects to hear the other's input. Or when one of you bows out from participating in the conversation at all. Listen up, financial nerds: Don't keep the financial details all to yourselves. And we would advise you to avoid acting like a know-it-all while using your "knowledge" to boss around your free-spirited spouse. And if you're the more carefree spouse, don't just nod your head and say, "That looks great, dear." You both have a vote and a voice in the budgeting or finance meetings. For couples who are new to this process, actually setting up a "business meeting" to talk through finances and budgeting can be enormously helpful—at a time when you can ensure that you're free of distractions. And if you're reluctant, just be reminded that you're both on the same team, so budgeting is something that has to be done together, rather than one of you taking this task on exclusively, as that can lead to all sorts of resentment and power imbalances. We'll discuss exercises later that can help with this process.

For now, let's do a closer examination of our couples.

Leticia and Kai: Mild Relationship Symptoms Related to Money and Finances

Leticia first came in alone and talked about how Kai's "frivolous" money spending threatened everything she had worked so hard for. She had endured a tough background. The oldest daughter of a single mother with four more daughters, she has had to fight for an education and then for economic stability. When she met Kai, she was thirty-two and had worked days and nights to create her own bakery and coffee shop that was a neighborhood hit. Kai was thirty-four and also had a small-business background, but, unlike Leticia, he had parents who made enough money to help him pay for college and help him establish his career. His degree in mechanical engineering had paved the way to a job at a very large manufacturing company, and he was on a path toward better positions there. He and Leticia fell in love, and when he asked her to marry him, she wanted to say yes but was afraid to risk her economic independence and security by being in a legal relationship with another person. Leticia was thrilled with Kai but, at the same time, terrified. Her mother had lost some of her (already scarce) money by loaning money to a boyfriend, who took off with it, and she had told Leticia never, ever to entrust her economic survival to a man. Thus Leticia put off marrying Kai for several years. Kai got increasingly restless and said either they were going to get married or he was going to end their relationship.

Ultimately, they did get married, but Leticia has never been comfortable with Kai about money. For example, he assumed that when they got married, everything of his belonged to his wife and vice versa. He said, "Everything I have is yours," and wanted one bank account and joint ownership of everything. Leticia, however, had worked hard to be independent and self-sufficient and didn't feel comfortable blending everything together. In addition, while she admired Kai's career success, she felt he spent money on things that were a waste (expensive dinners, fancy hotels, lottery tickets) and she always believed they could save more rather than spend more. She never quite relaxed about money even though they both now had quite good incomes. They fought about how much to put on a credit card, whether to use credit cards at all, how much to spend on a car, and even how the heat in the house should be regulated and whether to leave lights on during the day. For his part, Kai varied between being slightly and greatly annoyed with her—and sometimes he was just insulted. He would occasionally go out to buy a big-ticket item just to show he could. This act would send Leticia into hysterics. She would then want to separate "her" money and "his" money because she felt he endangered her security. Kai was having none of it.

Their conversations would go like this: Leticia would argue, "I don't see why we must put our accounts together. I know it's traditional, but I'm not traditional and I don't want to do it. We can do one household account. That's all that is necessary now." Kai would respond, "Marriage is putting everything together—taking on life together. Whatever we have, it should be together. Keeping anything separate feels like planning for divorce. The fact that you don't want to put things together makes me feel like you don't trust me. And if you don't trust me, what kind of marriage can we have?" They would carry on for a while, and then the conversation would eventually escalate when Leticia would say, "You are stupid about money. You throw it away. We will end up poor. I have struggled too hard to let you ruin my life." Kai would respond, "You are acting crazy. We are fine! You want to squeeze all the joy out of life. You want to control me, and I'm not going to let you do that."

Lars and Peter: Moderate Relationship Symptoms Related to Money and Finances

Money represents more than figuring out how much we have to spend or save. It can represent feeling good about ourselves, what we've accomplished, even what we deserve. Rob Becker, a comedian, used to do a bit called "Defending the Caveman," referencing that men were hunters and women were gatherers . . . and asserted that it is still true today! As a man, he thinks of something he needs, goes in and gets it, and is done. But women, in his opinion, are gatherers: They go in somewhere, they look around, they gather this, they gather that. And who knows what they will come out with. It's a funny comedy bit. But there is some truth to it—not by gender, we think, but maybe by typology. Some of us are hunters (we see what we want and get it as quickly as possible), and others are gatherers (we take time to find the best fruits and the best items). Some of us shop just to get what we need, and not only do we not love shopping, but we also try to get it over with as soon as possible. But for others, shopping *is* therapy. It makes us feel better, and we can let it get out of hand, both in terms of time spent (sometimes hours online or in T.J. Maxx) and sometimes the amount of money spent. In Peter's case, shopping is definitely a way to deal with pressure, with anxiety, and with his sense of doing well in the world. The problem is, at least to Lars, that the practice has become compulsive—therefore out of control—and has nothing to do with need and maybe not even so much with the objects bought. Peter will go out and get his fifth black turtleneck sweater. He will get another fancy watch. He will purchase a splurge gift (like getting all their cars' seats redone in leather to surprise Lars).

This process is very foreign to Lars. He is a minimalist. If he has one pair of dress pants and one pair of jeans, he feels that is enough. If Peter goes out and gets him a "gift" that he has already said he doesn't need, he returns it (if he can). That sparks another fight because Peter feels rejected when Lars doesn't want Peter's gifts. This became a major issue between them when Peter's purchases began to outstrip their ability to fully pay their credit card at the end of the month. The fact that Lars is now having to pay interest on overage makes him white-hot mad, and Peter is responding in kind with annoyance and giving Lars the cold shoulder.

Margo and Jack: Severe Relationship Symptoms Related to Money and Finances

Marriages are built on trust. Each partner, as we have talked about in earlier chapters, has to believe that he or she is safe with the other—physically, emotionally, and even financially. The partners share secrets, vulnerabilities, and even shame that has dogged them in the past. They are also supposed to be a team that survives better together than it does apart. When that turns out not to be true, on almost any dimension, it is a crisis. Margo did not know that Jack already had a gambling problem when she married him, and he did not tell her because he thought he had controlled it and he didn't want to scare her off. He occasionally engaged in sports betting with his friends, which she knew about and didn't think was a big deal, as a lot of their friends would bet on big events like March Madness or the Super Bowl. But when he was under stress, Jack would stop by the casino and play the slots or the roulette wheel for a while, and pretty soon he was back at more expensive games, playing blackjack or poker and doing more online gaming—maxing out his credit cards to try to win back what he had lost. When Margo uncovered debt-collection notices, she went into his office and found out more about how much debt they really had and how he had drained much of their savings. She was devastated. It wasn't just the debt, though that was important to her; it was the long trail of lies and Jack's refusal to talk about it. She explains, "When Jack was out of town, I hired a forensic computer guy to find out about these hidden cards and accounts. I had to treat my own husband like a criminal. It was humiliating, and I don't really know how to come back from this."

RELATIONSHIP Rx FOR EACH COUPLE

Couple: Leticia and Kai

Prescription: Relationship Vitamins: Get Naked, Financially Naked; Value of a Dollar

When there is a disagreement about how much to save and how much to spend, it causes continuing conflict over even the smallest purchases. This can become a bigger problem unless it is attended to. So what Leticia and

Kai had to do was get a real sense of their total financial picture in order to know what they could and couldn't afford, and how much they should save, and have real knowledge in order to create an economic plan they could live with. In order to prevent financial conflict in committed relationships, we need to have all our cards on the table and be open to becoming financially "naked." Just like getting naked with our partners for the first time, getting financially naked can bring its own share of trepidation and insecurity. In full disclosure, this is an exercise that Dr. Jessica found difficult to do personally—but after she and her partner completed it, she felt so much better, and the reward for her was a massive sense of relief.

Get Naked, Financially Naked

Getting financially naked is an exercise that is going to take a bit of time individually. It goes like this: Each partner makes a net-worth statement in which you list all your assets (savings accounts, cards that are paid off, equity in your homes, retirement accounts, etc.) and all your debts (student loans, car loans, mortgages, credit cards, etc.). You then, in order to have a conversation about a reasonable budget, make a list of income sources (i.e., how much you make per week or month) and regular expenses (phones, haircuts, day care, groceries, etc.). Some expenses may need to be monitored over time, or you may have to look back over the last year so you can come up with an average.

The two of you can then find a time—set aside a few hours—to go over your net-worth statements and the information you gathered for your budget. We have had some couples who decided to make a weekend out of it and booked a couple nights in a hotel—with half the time for "business" and half for pleasure. For those who would prefer not to use a good old-fashioned ledger sheet in your planning, you can utilize many free net-worth or budgeting tools and financial tools that are available online or as apps. Here are a few we like:

- https://www.bankrate.com/calculators/smart-spending/personal-net-worth-calculator.aspx
- https://www.nerdwallet.com/blog/finance/net-worth-calculator/

- https://www.kiplinger.com/tool/saving/T063-S001-net-worth -calculator-how-to-calculate-net-worth/index.php
- https://www.nfcc.org/resources/planning-tools-and-calculators /monthly-budget-planner/
- https://mint.intuit.com

After you have been financially naked with each other, it's time to talk about what money actually means to you. That's where the Value of a Dollar exercise comes in.

Value of a Dollar

Each person has a sheet of paper. Each person independently writes, "Money is to me . . ." and "Money means to me . . ." and completes these sentences. This process might result in a short list or a lengthy one for each partner. Then share each other's lists and take turns hearing each other's explanations of what money is or means to each of you, discussing the values each of you places on money. This conversation often reveals information couples had no idea about and will shed light on how you and your partner might handle dividing up money or tackling your financial concerns together. For example, in doing this exercise, Leticia was able to see that Kai valued fun and sponta- neity but also that, for him, putting money together meant trust and commit- ment. Kai was able to see that Leticia values security and self-sufficiency. He also gained a better understanding that she still had fears about money disap- pearing and that she was nervous she would be back where she started from, and he was able to see how important it was for her to have her own money. In sharing their lists and having the resulting conversation, they developed more compassion for each other and were able to figure out a compromise. In this case, Leticia and Kai (as we've advised many couples with similar conflicts to do) decided on three separate accounts: mine, yours, and ours. Their indi- vidual accounts were theirs to do with what they wished. Kai could use his account to live large when he felt like it; Leticia would have her own account to save her money as she wished. Their joint account was for the household expenses, gas, groceries, and date nights together. After becoming financially naked, they were able to look at each of their incomes and come up with a proportion (e.g., 30–60 percent) of their paychecks that made sense to put into their joint account. This number will vary for each couple and may have to be revisited over time as circumstances change.

Most of the time, it's not the money that's the issue. It's the difference in values that we attach to money. Part of an exercise like this one is getting away from looking for rational arguments to settle a money question and validating a partner's feelings by coming up with a solution that makes those feelings (and, in this case, fears) validated. This exercise makes each person feel better understood by his or her partner, like "OK, you get me!" Then a solution can be made by creating a plan that, for example, makes Leticia feel safer and more secure and Kai not feel rejected or untrustworthy.

Couple: Lars and Peter

Prescription: Relationship Medicine: Spending Freeze; Setting a Date— With a Financial Planner; Spending Caps; Planning for the Future; Optional Individual Therapy

Spending Freeze

The consequences for a marriage increase when spending habits greatly outstrip the ability to pay bills. In the case of Peter and Lars, Peter had made spending such a hobby that it was endangering their credit score, along with their peace of mind. In this case, the financial bleeding had to be stopped, immediately. First, they needed to issue a spending freeze in which they spent money only on essential items (bills, groceries, gas, etc.) until they were able to consult with a professional.

Setting a Date—With a Financial Planner

In this instance, their Relationship Medicine first involved setting up a meeting with a financial planner who could take the burden off Lars so he didn't have to be a nag and who could be an authority for Peter to listen to and not make it a relationship battle. Sometimes a decision needs objective data—and an objective ear and voice. Going to a financial planner can help a couple create a joint plan, as well as individual plans. Financial planners are not psychologists, but they know how difficult money matters can be in relationships and can be talented at finding compromises that help the family money work for the couple and also at creating a plan that can help maintain some economic independence. Be sure to find someone whose job it is to understand how you organize and spend your money and who can offer advice on spending, paying down debt, and budgeting, as opposed to someone who is selling you various investments. Financial planners can often be accessed through one's employer at little to no cost as part of your employee benefit or Employee Assistance Program (EAP). There are also many investment advisors who will offer a free consultation to you prior to signing up for an ongoing relationship.

Spending Caps

We often advise couples to set a limit of how much they can individually spend before consulting with each other on the purchase. For some couples, it's anything over $50; for other couples, it may be higher (e.g., $200 or $400) depending on their income and net worth. This approach allows some flexibility and freedom for the partner who is the spender, as well as peace of mind for the partner who prefers to save. Peter and Lars decided that they would set a limit of $100, and anything over that needed to be discussed ahead of time.

Planning for the Future

In this exercise, each partner writes down both a five-year plan and a retirement-vision plan.[4] In each of these plans, you will answer the following questions.

Five-year plan:

- Where do you want to be in five years when it comes to your career?
- Where do you want to be in five years when it comes to where you and your partner live?
- Where do you want to be in five years when it comes to your lifestyle?
- Where do you want to be in five years when it comes to your family life?
- Where do you want to be in five years when it comes to work/life balance?

Retirement-vision plan:

- What age do you want to retire?
- Where do you want to live?
- What do you expect life to look like?
- What does your time together look like as a couple?
- What does your time together look like as a family?

Each of you will share your responses with the other. Answering these questions and having these conversations will shed light on what each of you values regarding planning for the future—and realizing that a lot of what you dream for has a financial price tag and/or financial sacrifices or choices that you'll have to make. By having a clear sense of what each of you wants, you can work toward a compromise or shared goals together. For Peter and Lars, they were able to take their answers back to their financial planner, who helped them develop a strategy for the next five years and keep in mind their wishes for retirement.

Optional Individual Therapy

If Peter was unable to control his spending, this situation might also need a therapist because Peter was using money to self-soothe and he needed another mechanism to do that. While it might be instructive for both members of the couple to find counselors, it was probably Peter who had to do the initial work on himself to find out why spending money was his way of calming himself. Then, when he got a better handle on what was a bad habit, he could figure out how to develop another way of burning off tension that didn't put the couple's financial health in jeopardy.

Couple: Margo and Jack

Prescription: Relationship CPR: Work with a Therapist; Enlist the Help of a Financial Planner to Address Debt

When betrayal and manipulation have created a perilous situation for couples financially and emotionally, the relationships become fragile from both the fear and the lies themselves. Jack and Margo were facing real financial problems from Jack's clear addiction to gambling and a loss of trust because, as often happens in addiction, he became successful at covering his tracks for so long. That is the problem with a real addiction: The people struggling with addiction know they are stuck in the grip of it, but they don't want to be discovered because they feel guilty and mired in a mess that they may still believe they have control over or can solve. Addiction is a disease—whether it's drug addiction, alcoholism, or gambling addiction. Going cold turkey is, for the most part, not possible. There is no healthy solution without dealing with the addiction head on, so at this point, if there is any hope of saving the relationship, the wise choice is to go to a licensed therapist skilled in working with addiction. This professional could help Jack explore his past experiences and deeper fears and find the reasons for his behaviors. The therapist could also help Margo understand how addictions start and how they truly become diseases affecting areas of the brain—and that while it doesn't excuse his bad behavior, it helps explain it. Margo may be able to increase her empathy for her husband and see his betrayal as the act of someone struggling with a disease as opposed to someone being a "bad person." A solid therapist may also be able to unearth some feelings that allow for more self-understanding and understanding of each other and help create the possibility of finding a personalized plan to see whether there can be a future for the relationship. Additionally, Jack and Margo could consider seeking out groups for addiction at https://www.gamblersanonymous.org/ga/ or, for those who care for those struggling with gambling addiction, at https://www.gam-anon .org. Couples can also contact the National Council on Problem Gambling at 1-800-522-4700 or review online resources, including resources to help find outpatient or inpatient treatment, on the National Problem Gambling Helpline page at https://www.ncpgambling.org/help-treatment/national -helpline-1-800-522-4700/.

Summary

All three couples have shown us that money isn't just a piece of paper—it's often one of the hottest topics for couples and yet one of the most difficult ones to talk about! Money influences so much of what we do in our lives in the present and in the future—whether it's figuring out what credit card to pay off this week, whether the kids can join camps this summer, or where we want to retire in the distant future. If we aren't on the same page with our partners when it comes to finances, there is inevitably going to be conflict. By increasing our communication about money and finances, coupled with having the right tools and resources, we can avoid financial crises or major disputes in our relationships.

10

FRIENDS AND FAMILY

Why do we always spend the holidays with her family? She always picks her family's side over mine. My mother-in-law is a monster-in-law. He spends more time with his friends than he does with our family! I feel really jealous about one of my partner's friends. She's spending way too much time with her coworkers, and I'm worried she's telling them too much about our business.

As everyone knows, you can't pick your family; you can pick only your friends. But that isn't quite true, is it? You certainly can't pick who gave birth to you or who your parents were when you were growing up, but you can learn how to modify your exposure (or your reaction) to any bad behavior they might throw your way. We're not saying doing that is easy, but, as we will discuss in this chapter, it can be necessary—especially when absorbing bad family behavior is having a negative impact on your relationship.

And let's not let friends off the hook either. While you can pick your friends, your partner may not have had a say in whom you chose or whom you hung out with as a kid and kept friendships going with based on how close you were in middle school. While your spouse might like or even admire many of your friends, there may be one or two who he or she feels is unsupportive of the marriage or maybe just annoying or, worse, creepy. You might even agree with your partner to a point—and that point is that you still want to keep those friends even if your partner is not happy about it. You may even know that your friend is "not to everyone's taste," but you've learned to appreciate your friend, and you are not ready to sever the friendship.

Social connectedness, in the form of strong bonds with friends and family members, helps to buffer us from stress and to support our resilience—including the resilience of our marriages. While family and friends can be a real blessing to a marriage, it is equally true that they may be so disruptive that we have to make new ground rules or set substantial boundaries for socializing that may even include protecting our partners from interacting with them. Some of the biggest fights couples may have involve the inclusion or exclusion of family members or friends whom one partner loves, likes, or at least tolerates while the other partner doesn't want those people around at all.

In talking about how to handle conflict regarding friends or family, there are three guiding questions to think about applying:

1. How central is this person to the partner's life?
2. How toxic is this person to either individual or to the marriage?
3. Is there mutual agreement about this person or the person's impact? Or does one partner see this person quite differently?

Why are these questions important? Because even if this person is doing real damage, it may be necessary to help the partner who is holding onto the relationship see not only the bad behavior but also how it affects the other partner or the marriage. Further, figuring out how central the person is to the partner's life (e.g., a close sibling or a best friend versus a high school acquaintance) may result in a more carefully thought-out plan and certainly a more sensitive discussion.

Let's take a look at three couples struggling with issues related to friends and family.

Couple #1: Maddy and Dylan: Mild Relationship Symptoms Related to Friends and Family

Maddy and Dylan have been married for three years after living together for two years. They are a happy couple most of the time, and Maddy likes most of Dylan's friends. However, she hates his "boys' nights," during which, at least once per week, Dylan's friends go to one of the friends' houses, smoke cigars, drink a lot of beer, play poker, and ultimately get plastered. Most of the time after one of these evenings, Dylan is too drunk to drive home, so he ends up spending the night, and when the group is at Maddy and Dylan's apartment, there are usually a couple of drunk guys sleeping it off in their living room the next morning. Maddy is angry about it almost weekly and believes Dylan prioritizes his friends over spending time with her and Dylan's extended families. At the same time, Dylan says that his friends are "my boys" and it's the only time during the week when he gets to let loose and blow off steam after a stressful work week.

Couple #2: Charlotte and Garth: Moderate Relationship Symptoms Related to Friends and Family

Charlotte has serious mother-in-law problems. Garth has a mother who is intrusive—both physically and emotionally. She stops by whenever she feels like it, and, because Garth has given her a key, she lets herself in without calling or asking Charlotte whether it's OK. When there is tension between Charlotte and her mother-in-law, Garth, who has always been extremely close with his mother, tells Charlotte to be the "bigger person" and be nicer to his mother. Yet his mother is constantly disruptive and demeaning to Charlotte.

Couple #3: Nicolette and Ed: Severe Relationship Symptoms Related to Friends and Family

Nicolette is furious with Ed because he has refused to stop being friends with a woman, Layla, whom he had an affair with at work many years ago. Nicolette knows from mutual friends that Layla has been privy to information about her and Ed's marriage and has spread stories about humiliating parts of the ups and downs of their marriage, and she has said terrible things about Ed's sexual issues to various friends and acquaintances. Nicolette feels exposed and humiliated, but Ed refuses to believe that Layla has said these things about either him or Nicolette. Nicolette is not sure whether there is something more going on with Layla and Ed, but she knows that Layla is not a real friend to either of them.

Friends and family, while they can provide a tremendous amount of support to a marriage, can sometimes be a source of conflict—and all three of our couples are experiencing the negative impact of outside relationships on their own relationships. With communication and the right tools and supports, all three couples could address their conflicts and prioritize their marriages in a way in which each partner is satisfied.

Numerous studies have shown that healthy relationships, including those with friends and family members, are good for our brains and our overall well-being.[1] Social relationships also matter when it comes to resiliency because they help us feel less stress when we are suffering. How resilient we are may have as much to do with our external supports from others as it does with our internal makeups (like our temperaments or perseverance). Social relationships provide resources such as financial support, a helping hand with tasks of life, emotional support, and assistance with problem-solving—making it easier to face challenges. In a large-scale report on resilience, the American Psychological Association reported that the primary factor in resilience is having caring and supportive relationships within and outside the family.[2] When we're in trouble, we naturally turn to others, which is why it is important to have not just a healthy marriage but also healthy familial ties and other forms of social connection.

In marriages, friends and family can serve many roles, including providing support to couples, creating more opportunities for shared experiences, and providing new or expanded networks for our partners to rely on in times of need. And maintaining healthy relationships with other couples protects our relationships with our partners and can make us more attractive to our partners!

When you get married or find your long-term partner, it's natural that your other relationships are going to be impacted in significant ways. It's important, for the sake of your marriage, that you continue to nourish the parts of your life that made you who you were before you met your partner. Hobbies, talents, and friends all are aspects of life that allow you to continue growing your own sense of self separate from your partner. Having your own sense of self—including your own relationships and connections outside the marriage—can actually attract your partner to you more! We see so often that people drop friendships just because they are in serious relationships or are getting married. While such relationships may no longer be the top priority in your life, they do represent an important part of who you are, can be a buffer to stress, and allow you space to be and grow separately from your partner.

So here's the deal. We know that you pick your friends—you don't pick your family. When you get married, you inherit your partner's family (for better or worse) and you also inherit your partner's friends, but these are friends you didn't get to pick. Thus, there are many common conflicts that emerge related to navigating relationships with family and friends, which may include the following:

- Where to spend the holidays and with whom
- In-laws who may be opinionated or disrespectful
- Jealousy over relationships with certain friends or coworkers
- Hurt feelings if a partner seems to be prioritizing friendships or other family relationships over the marriage
- Resentment at not spending enough time with friends or family
- Family or friends not liking you (or your partner) or vice versa

Sometimes working through issues related to friends and family involves identifying where the resentment is coming from and having concrete discussions about priorities. Resentment can build if we're not getting our own needs for social connection met. Resentment can also build if we feel like our partners are prioritizing other social connections over us. We have only so much time in the day between work, life, and all our responsibilities—it's hard to create time for others as well as our partners. Thus, it's important to figure out what (or who) our priorities are and how we and our partners can support each other in having the family and social connections we desire.

There are some basic ground rules that can prevent so many friends-and-family problems from impacting our relationships. These ground rules focus on setting boundaries around our marriages or long-term relationships. We lovingly but strongly suggest the following:

- Avoid making disparaging remarks about your partner in front of your friends or family.
- Have each other's backs in public with your friends and family.
- If you have complaints about your partner and need to talk, find a small number of trusted people you can do this with—people who support

you individually and as a couple—and allow your partner to do the same. Just make sure you don't keep secrets about this from each other.

- Don't underestimate the power of a planned conversation with family or friends to problem-solve and make your boundaries clear.

Lastly, when it comes to that oh-so-uncomfortable feeling of jealousy and friendships, we have a few thoughts. Unpacking jealousy and what contributes to it requires having uncomfortable conversations and setting expectations. Jealousy is a normal human emotion. We all will experience it—even Beyoncé and Brad Pitt feel jealous. Those who have more anxious attachment styles will have much higher rates of jealousy and will struggle with this feeling more than others. However, jealousy responds well to both cognitive processing and reassurance from partners, as well as expectation setting. We could use the Cognitive Triangle (as discussed in chapter 2) to address distorted thoughts we might have (e.g., "She's going to leave me for someone else she spends time with"). Keep in mind that jealousy may also be a cue that something isn't quite right, so talk about this subject with your partner. Conversations will need to focus on what you and your partner are comfortable or not comfortable with and coming up with ground rules and expectations. For example, you could be uncomfortable with late nights out at conferences, so have a ground rule that you call or text each other when you are back home for the night. Or, if there is a particular person you feel jealous about, have a ground rule that your partner does not go out for drinks with that person without you, does not go out with that person at all, or makes sure to talk to you about it in advance. Each couple will have to do what they feel works best for them in their relationship.

Now let's do a closer examination of our couples.

Maddy and Dylan: Mild Relationship Symptoms Related to Friends and Family

Maddy and Dylan have been arguing about Dylan's boys' nights for so long that Dylan just considers it part of Maddy's "OCD" concern about the living room getting messy and her "princess" dislike of what he thinks is typical guy behavior. What Dylan has never truly accepted as real or worthy of consideration is Maddy's distress at having her house "invaded" and her fear that one of these days Dylan will have serious health problems from all the drinking and smoking. The whole idea of drinking until being drunk not only annoys her but also worries her. Additionally, she is hurt that Dylan won't modify—much less eliminate—a habit that bothers her so much. Meanwhile, Dylan feels that Maddy is a buzzkill, and he is embarrassed when his friends joke with him around the poker table about his "curfew." Maddy is upset because she'd like to spend more time with her family, but Dylan's boys' nights often take over their weekends—especially holiday weekends. Dylan doesn't seem to care what they do for holiday weekends, but Maddy thinks they should be spending time with her family or his family by hosting for the holidays instead of Dylan spending them with his friends and recovering for the rest of the weekend on the couch.

Charlotte and Garth: Moderate Relationship Symptoms Related to Friends and Family

Charlotte feels like the backup quarterback in her own home—her mother-in-law calls all the shots and Garth lets her get away with it. The hard truth is that Garth is more married to his mother than his wife, and his mother knows it. She is unwilling to stop being the most important person in his life, and, in many ways, it is understandable. He is her only son (her daughter has moved away, out of the state), and she is trying to establish her centrality in his life by not observing that his home is the domain of him and his wife. She is trying to show that it is part of her rightful territory, and he is letting her do that. This is not an uncommon dynamic—it's hard for many mothers to let go of their children when they get married—but letting go is a rite of passage, and if they don't do it, it can be disastrous for everyone.

Why does Garth let his mother take over and mistreat his wife? Most likely, it could be a mix of love and guilt with just a touch of cowardice. His mother raised him and, as a single mother, made so many sacrifices for him, and he is immensely grateful. She's always been extremely involved in his life; he doesn't know any different. He loves his mother, and she is alone. He believes she behaves this way because she loves him so much that her identity has involved her taking care of him all his life, and because she's lonely. How can he tell her no?

Meanwhile, the complete access he allows his mother to have to their home is telling his wife she is in second place, and that hurts and infuriates Charlotte. Further, Garth's mother does not show proper respect for Charlotte. She drops hints about how the house looks dirty or that Charlotte needs to have her roots done on her hair, or she makes comments about what Charlotte is cooking that night for dinner, such as it being too fatty or not enough for her son. Garth's mother has even brought meals over without checking what Charlotte is making (even when she's already made dinner!) because "you never make my son's favorite tuna casserole, so I just thought I'd help make this dinner special." Her treatment of Charlotte has also been affecting their children. For example, their nine-year-old has said to Garth, "Grandma isn't nice to Mom. I told Mom that I liked her cooking because I think her feelings were hurt when Grandma threw out the mac and cheese." Clearly, some boundaries must be established, but ideally without too much of a mother-in-law meltdown.

Nicolette and Ed: Severe Relationship Symptoms Related to Friends and Family

It is not clear whether Ed is having a physical affair with Layla, but he is definitely having an emotional one. He has created a triangle with another woman, and that woman does not support him in the way that true friends do. A friend does not make fun of you, does not tell humiliating stories about you that you have entrusted to them confidentially, and certainly does not try to undermine your marriage. Layla is circulating criticisms of Nicolette, and she is privy to some of the most intimate parts of Nicolette's marriage to Ed. Using those facts for her own pleasure by gossiping about Nicolette and Ed in an unkind way, Layla is betraying both Ed and Nicolette, but Ed's ego is blinding him to what is really going on. He was once Layla's lover, and based on the way he acts, it is fair for Nicolette to be suspicious that something is still going on. Even if it isn't still a sexual relationship, the fact that Layla has spread intimate rumors about Nicolette and Ed's marriage that are circulating in their friendship group is cause enough for Nicolette to be embarrassed and enraged. Nicolette was recently told by a colleague about some very disparaging remarks Layla made about her and Ed (calling her a "dead fish" in bed who wasn't able to have an orgasm and saying that Ed struggled with premature ejaculation) when this colleague took Layla out on a first date. The colleague was shocked, and despite the risk of embarrassing Nicolette, he felt that she needed to know.

When Nicolette heard some of the information Layla gave before the colleague could interrupt Layla and tell her to stop, Nicolette realized that the details were so personal they must have come from Ed. Who else would know that she and Ed have had arguments about their sex life? She hadn't told a soul! Worse yet, that colleague was not the only person who could give a sordid account of Nicolette's most private moments with her husband. She even heard about how she and Ed were made fun of in Layla's book group.

RELATIONSHIP Rx FOR EACH COUPLE

Couple: Maddy and Dylan

Prescription: Relationship Vitamins: "What Are We Really Fighting About?" and Reflective Listening; Share Your Top Ten; Holiday Calendar

"What Are We Really Fighting About?" and Reflective Listening

This exercise can be helpful to uncover the root of the problem and determine what couples are actually in conflict over. The issue with Maddy and Dylan may have had to do with her concerns about his drinking, the condition of the home, her feeling neglected in the marriage, all of the above, or something else altogether. The "What Are We Really Fighting About?" exercise involves couples describing what they see as the issue and how they feel about it and then working toward a solution. First, each person on their own describes what the argument is about and how they feel about it.

For example, Maddy's list may have included any of the following:

- I am upset that you get drunk and pass out—it makes me scared you will hurt yourself or do something stupid.
- I am worried because I don't think these guys are a good influence on you.
- I hate losing control of my living room.
- I am left with a mess and that destroys my sense of control over my living room.

- I hate the smell of beer that pervades the house and the noise that makes it impossible for me to sleep when you are here.
- We have so little time together, and I am jealous that I lose so many nights to your friends.
- I don't get to have my family over on the weekends as much as I'd like because either your friends are here or the house smells bad—or you're hungover.
- We don't get to spend holidays hosting our families or visiting with families because you seem to be prioritizing your friends over them.

Dylan's list could include any of the following:

- I don't think it's too much to ask to have one night a week with my buddies doing whatever I want to do.
- I feel overcontrolled and I don't like you trying to control me.
- I feel torn. This is really about you not liking my friends, and these are my good friends.
- Just because you don't like cards or drinking doesn't mean you get to tell me not to do it.
- You don't realize that you spend time with your friends more than I see my friends.
- It's important for me to be able to blow off steam with my friends at the end of the week.
- I like beer and I only drink too much when we have boys' nights—it's not like I do it every night when it's just us, and I feel badly that you paint me out to be an alcoholic or something.

Then share your lists with each other and talk about those feelings. If there is a misunderstanding, try to correct what may not be true. Then use the Reflective Listening Strategy discussed in chapter 2 to each fully understand the other's position. That brings us to step two.

After you've talked through each other's positions and have a better understanding of each other's feelings, think about ways you might compromise. Keep in mind that in negotiations or compromises, you're not trying to get everything you want; rather, you're coming to a plan that you both can live with. Each of you then, on your own, brainstorms things you could do differently that could move this problem to a doable, reasonable solution. Then present your options to each other, and the two of you decide together on a solution (or combination of solutions) that makes sense and then agree that this plan will settle the matter.

Here's an example of what Maddy and Dylan could do.

Possibilities from Dylan:

- I promise to take an Uber there and back so if I am drinking too much, I won't stay over.
- I promise not to drink to the point that I can't drive (no more than one beer per hour).
- I won't have the guys over here.
- I will make new ground rules for over here regarding the mess and cigar smoke or whatever else bothers you; we can create them together.
- I promise to have one date night per week to make sure we also get quality time.

Possibilities from Maddy:

- I will get over my upset when they are here if they leave by __ o'clock.
- I will be happy to have them here in the summer but not the winter so that it all happens outside in the yard and not in the house.
- I can deal with the poker night if you never drink so much you have to stay over, or if you always take an Uber there and are back before __ o'clock.
- I understand your need to connect with your buddies, so let's deal with the cigar smoke and alcohol in the following ways:
  - Move the cigar smoking to the basement or outdoors.
  - Keep recycling and trash bins nearby to toss out the containers.
  - Stop drinking at X number of drinks.
- I can deal with it most of the time if you can miss it occasionally for important things that come up in our lives.
- Can you cut back to once or twice per month instead of every week?

The important thing was to stop an issue that was happening predictably every week and took up space in their heads and their marriage, rent free. While this issue may have seemed small, it was the type that was way more powerful than one would think. Getting rid of this conflict at the Vitamins level would have a bigger benefit than they thought. It would reduce or stop bickering, which psychotherapist and podcaster Esther Perel has called "low intensity chronic warfare," which ultimately takes a toll on the relationship because it undermines comfort in the home and erodes partners' respect for each other.[3]

Share Your Top Ten

One of the issues that comes up in relationships is not fully understanding who all the players are in each other's lives and those people's significance. We may think we know our partners' closest relationships, but we may not truly understand why our partners care so much about those relationships. This exercise, a very simple one, can help open up the communication about important relationships in a way that allows each of you to ensure that you are supporting your partner's meaningful relationships. Each partner writes down his or her top-ten most important relationships, making sure to put each other at the top of the lists. The second part of this exercise is to explain *why*. Tell each other what you value about each person on the list, how he or she is supportive to you, and what you enjoy about him or her. The lists can include family members, friends, or even close coworkers or other meaningful people.

Holiday Calendar

Holidays are usually a hot-button topic for families—it's not a bad thing to be wanted in more than one place. This is a topic, though, that we advise addressing well in advance of each holiday. Couples can take out a calendar ahead of time and talk about what is important to them and determine what may be fair. Couples can take turns alternating each year, trade holidays or offer to host, or even choose holidays that you decide will be spent with just the two of you or with your kids—there are a lot of strategies. If you are announcing that you're not coming to Christmas, it's best to have a consolation prize in your pocket like "We'll be there for XYZ holiday" or "Next year we will make the trip." If you live close to one extended family, you may have Sunday dinner with your family every week, but your partner does not get to see his or her family as much. In those instances, it's important that you frequently make an effort to be sure your partner knows he or she is supporting your family relationship (prioritizing holidays, etc.).

Couple: Charlotte and Garth

Prescription: Relationship Medicine: Planned Conversation; Consultation with a Professional

Planned Conversation

This is a strategy to use when a couple is struggling with issues involving third parties (such as Garth's mother) outside their relationship. The idea is to schedule a meeting with the third person or party to set a boundary and have an honest and direct conversation stating your feelings and your needs. This can be done if there is increasing conflict or boundary violations, as a way to set boundaries and expectations. The idea is to work toward a resolution; however, part of planning it out involves preparing one another for pushback or fallout. Prior to meeting with the third party, work together as a couple to have a plan for the meeting. As part of this plan, come up with a code word or gesture (e.g., a hand squeeze or pat on the knee). The code word could be an indication to your partner to soften his or her stance, or that you're getting upset, or that it's time to exit—or it could be just for reassurance. When meeting, approach the conversation as goal-directed and state your wish, such as "Our goal is to have a positive relationship with you and feel supported as a couple over the long term" or "Our goal is to spend time with you that feels good for everyone at this table and also to not have resentment against one another." Use "I feel" or "we feel" statements followed by stated needs. For example, Garth could say to his mother, "I feel upset and stressed out when you stop over without notice and criticize our home. I need you to call or text before you come over. I need you to stop making negative comments about Charlotte or our home." Family dynamics are strong, so expect pushback—don't allow the third party to blame the other partner or look for a scapegoat, which may happen when family members feel on the defense. Lastly, there are some situations in which you have to be very clear and concrete and set distinct and firm boundaries. There are also times when disengaging from toxic treatment of you or your partner needs to be done for your own well-being and the health of your marriage.

Consultation with a Professional

There are times when, even at the Medicine level, we want to bring on the expertise of a professional. If Garth was unable to set boundaries with his mother or entertain a planned conversation, this task might have required a third person. Garth obviously didn't understand or want to know how out of bounds his mother was—or if he did, he felt too constrained to do anything. His mother acted like a bully, and he cowered when it came to her. Charlotte might think that she was getting nowhere because this had been an established pattern for so long that Garth couldn't see a way out of it.

Therefore, taking action required going to a professional (e.g., licensed therapist, pastor) to whom each person could present his or her part of the story. Charlotte could discuss her hurt and her anger about relegation to second place in her husband's life. Garth could express that his mother only wanted to love him and, though she was intrusive, it was her way of showing love and he couldn't do anything about it without doing irreparable harm to her and to their relationship. As he said, "She's a lonely old woman, and I am the most important thing in her life. What am I going to do, destroy her?" His thinking might stand in a conversation between just him and Charlotte, but no therapist was going to side with him on this issue. The therapist or other professional unfortunately would have more standing here than his wife and could work with the couple to create more reasonable boundaries (e.g., changing the house locks or agreeing to no unannounced visits except perhaps during the holidays or maybe just on weekends—whatever felt comfortable to Charlotte).

The therapist could explain to Garth that not only had he put his wife into a difficult situation, but it was also the wrong model for his children, who could see how this situation hurt their mom and were already starting to say protective things about their mom when Grandma came over. If he saw that he was hurting his wife and hurting their relationship, as well as upsetting his kids, it might allow him to create some better boundaries with his mother.

Granted, whether it was having a planned conversation or working with a professional to set boundaries, Garth's mother wouldn't like it. But she would get over it because otherwise she would be given much less time with her son—or at least with her son in his home. The new boundaries could start out as modest: no keys to the house (or changing the locks) and stopping by on only weekends, for example. We can't work miracles, so it was unlikely we could stop all snarky comments, but if she berated Charlotte repeatedly and didn't observe the new rules, access to the home could get more exclusionary. Some people will respond to costs only, not to pleas or to any sense of respect that marriage deserves. Thus, there are times when just asking for a change without consequences isn't going to work. Sure, she was going to be angry at Garth, and especially Charlotte, but this was the time when Garth needed to draw another boundary and tell his mother that he didn't want to hear criticism about his wife. If she continued, he needed to disengage from her. If it went in that direction, it would be important for Garth to receive professional consultation to stay the course so he did not allow his guilt and decades of established patterns to override the decision he and his wife made to put a boundary around their marriage.

The dynamic between Garth and Charlotte, while not uncommon, was a serious situation. Although it was not quite at the CPR level, it needed immediate attention before Charlotte realized she would never be number one and became fed up and left.

Couple: Nicolette and Ed

Prescription: Relationship CPR: Couples Therapy; Gains and Losses Exercise; End the Non-Friendship

Couples Therapy

Nicolette and Ed were at a crisis point—one that seemed to have a relatively easy solution, though Ed was not able to see that. Thus it would be critical to work with a skilled couples therapist to unpack the answers to the many questions related to Nicolette and Ed's predicament. There were many questions to address, such as the following: Why would Ed trust Layla's denial of these facts when they were so easy to prove? Why would he trust his ex-girlfriend over his wife? Why would he tell Layla these very private stories?

Why didn't he want to protect Nicolette? All of this pointed to a marriage gone terribly wrong, and it was now unsafe, untrusting, unkind, and unstable. There was a third, destructive person in this marriage who had been given material to humiliate, embarrass, and potentially destroy Nicolette and Ed. It was not clear what there was to preserve, but if there was any chance, it would have to be worked on in therapy.

Gains and Losses

It had been very difficult for Ed to consider ending the friendship with Layla. For whatever reason, he had held onto this relationship, to the dismay of Nicolette and their mutual friends. It would be helpful for Ed to spend some time working on a Gains and Losses exercise. In this exercise, you write down what you will gain if you follow through with a decision such as disengaging from someone who may be toxic to your life. You also write down what you will lose. Then you compare the lists. Ed wrote down that he would gain "my wife's happiness," "my wife's trust," "more respect from my wife and friends," "less stress," and "no more feeling embarrassed in our friend group." He wrote down that he would "lose a confidant," "hurt Layla's feelings," "lose our special friendship together where I can tell her anything," and "lose Layla's respect." As he wrote down his lists, he was able to (with the help of his therapist) see that the "confidant" and "special friendship" he would lose could, and should, be qualities of another relationship he already had—his relationship with his wife. The therapist also pointed out that him "telling Layla anything" also resulted in her not keeping private information private—a sign of a toxic "friendship" and that she did not truly respect him if she shared his very private information with other people.

End the Non-Friendship

It is clear to us (and probably to you) that Layla was no friend to either of them, despite Ed's beliefs. Feeling humiliated and angry, Nicolette told Ed that he had to immediately stop talking to or seeing Layla; that would be an essential step if the marriage had any chance of repair. Ed equivocated, and Nicolette made an appointment with a divorce lawyer. Ed had begged her not to do that for his and their children's sake. However, he decided that he did not want to lose his marriage. It took Nicolette meeting with the lawyer and him realizing that his gains far outweighed his losses for him to agree to sever the relationship with Layla.

Summary

Friends and family can be enormous sources of support for couples—early in our relationships and years and decades later. As relationships are often complicated and priorities shift as couples commit to each other, family and friend systems can be disrupted. When the status quo is upended, sometimes bad behavior ensues. Whether it's mothers-in-law turned monsters-in-law, boys' nights taking over family time, or jealousy over exes, other people have the potential to upend our lives and our marriages or long-term commitments. There are some simple and effective strategies that can be utilized to protect our marriages, as well as preserve our friendships and family relationships. For all three of our couples, addressing conflict regarding friends and family involved difficult but necessary conversations and boundary setting.

11

CHILDREN AND PARENTING

Being a parent isn't what I thought it would be. I thought I would be an amazing dad until I had kids. I thought I would love being a parent—why am I so stressed or miserable much of the time? I don't know who I am anymore; I just feel like I'm "Mom" and nobody else. He doesn't seem that interested in spending time with me and the kids. I never thought I would let my kids eat sugary cereal, not take a bath every night before bed, [insert preconceived thought about being a perfect parent]. Why am I always the bad cop when she gets to be the good cop? She coddles the kids—they will never learn to do anything on their own! Our kids have taken over our lives.

As we mentioned earlier, having children does not just change our lives; it ends the lives that we had pre-kids. There is little room for spontaneity, it's harder to be sexy, and there is far less "us" time that does not also involve tiny people in the mix. There is a time when we learn the hard truth that the lives we had before are over and we now have new lives—and at some point we will grieve the lives we had before but at the same time embrace these loving, wild, sometimes chaotic lives we now have.

When talking with couples, there is nothing more personal than children—and nothing more emotionally charged. For most couples, having their first child introduces a new type of love—a love they've never known before. When we have our firstborns in our arms, we know we'll do whatever it takes to keep them safe and happy. Dr. Jessica says that when her son was born, it felt like her heart jumped out of her body and was running around in someone else's—a love that was intense and powerful, but also scary and fraught with a whole new set of worries. Despite the love, despite our best intentions, parenting introduces personal challenges we never anticipated. It is a massive adjustment and a challenge that no couple who has children is spared. We could do an entire book series just on parenting, so we cannot do it justice with one chapter—however, we would be remiss if we wrote a book on relationships and left out one of the most challenging topics for couples. We have found that when couples struggle with parenting, it typically has to do with three things: managing expectations, the past getting in the way of the present, and communication. So we will be reviewing some of what we discussed in earlier chapters.

Let's look at three couples who are also parents.

Couple #1: Tom and Mariana: Mild Relationship Symptoms Related to Children and Parenting

Tom and Mariana have been married for ten years and have two children, ages six and eight. Lately, they have been having disagreements regarding the workload in the home and about how to raise their kids, and it's causing stress for both of them.

Couple #2: Keanu and Kate: Moderate Relationship Symptoms Related to Children and Parenting

Keanu and Kate have been married for thirteen years. They have two children, ages seven and two. They have been sleeping in separate beds and have not spent time as just a couple in over two years, since Kate's second pregnancy. They love and respect each other but are essentially housemates passing in the night. Both of them are unhappy.

Couple #3: Brett and Tabitha: Severe Relationship Symptoms Related to Children and Parenting

Brett and Tabitha have been married for fifteen years and have three children, ages thirteen, eleven, and nine. Their relationship has been rocky over the years, with some very high highs but also very low lows—both of them thought having children would bring them closer together. Their conflict has escalated to the point that their children are struggling and forced to take sides.

All three of these couples struggle with unmet expectations and communication failures related to parenting. Although they are at various stages, they could all benefit from focused attention on their parenting—and prioritizing their marriages. With some focused, intentional conversations and a little homework, much of the conflict or turmoil related to parenting could be addressed or, if intervention had been done early on, could have been avoided in the first place.

As much as we'd like to believe this were true, children don't come with manuals. Dr. Jessica, who is a national expert in children and parenting, had read close to forty books on parenting prior to her first child being born. She remembers holding her son, who was a colicky baby described by his pediatrician as "spirited," and crying for an hour because she felt like a failure as a mother for not being able to soothe her child. She could not have been more prepared with knowledge, but what she wasn't prepared for was the emotional adjustment you have to make when you have children—that there aren't always apparent answers and much of parenting is trial and error. If we are in the middle of the parenting throes, inevitably there will be times when we don't feel as close to our partners as we did earlier in our relationships—we may feel like our relationships have gotten transactional in that the content of conversations centers around Jonny's naptimes or the kids' soccer schedules. We may feel less connected, or, when we do connect, we and our partners may be like business partners or roommates. We may say to ourselves, "When the kids get older, we will get back in sync," or "When the kids are older, we'll focus on us again." This is very dangerous thinking for a marriage. What ends up happening is that many parents hyper-focus on the children while neglecting the marriage, and the marriage erodes over time. We might be surprised to hear that the common notion "the children come first" is actually *not good for our children* or our families in the long run. This doesn't mean that the kids come last, but the kids can't be first because if they are first, then our marriages take a back seat. It is from the foundation of a rock-solid marriage that children can grow and thrive.

Seeing their parents in love and prioritizing each other, even if they balk at the notion of seeing their parents hug or kiss or prioritize date night, is actually calming for children. If we pour all our resources into our children while neglecting our spouses, fast-forward fifteen years and we'll be staring at strangers. There's a reason the divorce rate among couples over age fifty has more than doubled since the 1990s.[1]

You want what's best for your kids? The best thing you can do for your children is to prioritize your relationship—it's not selfish, and it does not mean you love your children less. When children see their parents communicating with respect and loving each other, including by showing physical affection, their own psychological security increases and you're more likely to have securely attached children who then grow up to have secure attachments in their own romantic relationships in adulthood.

There are a few parenting suggestions or ground rules for less conflict related to parenting. These may seem basic, but if they are ignored, more complicated parenting and marital issues can ensue.

1. Ensure that you and your partner are making parenting decisions together. If you don't agree, find a time to discuss it separate from the children. In those conversations, you want to ensure that you're listening to each other's opinions—reflective listening may be a strategy you try here too. You may want to come up with some sort of code word that a topic requires more conversation or something you can say to the kids, such as "Your father and I will talk about it and get back to you" or "This is something Mommy and I are going to decide together." It is natural for children to play one parent against the other. It's sort of a rite of passage as a kid—how am I going to get my needs or wants met? The challenge is for parents not to fall into that trap, and the only way to do that is to make sure you are aware that it's normal for kids to do that and to communicate with your partner. By ensuring that you are making parenting decisions together, you will prevent parenting disagreements from derailing your marriage.

2. Don't underestimate the importance of structure and routine. For kids, structure means predictability. Dr. Jessica talks a lot in her book for pediatricians about the importance of routines for parents and children.[2] If you have routines in the home, such as bedtime routines

with a set bedtime, everything else runs more smoothly. Predictability and consistency in the form of routines sends signals to the child's brain that he or she is safe—expectations and rules are good for kids! Make sure you pay attention to bedtime—have a set bedtime at night that is early enough to allow you and your partner to spend time with each other one on one before you fall asleep. (Until you have teenagers. Then all bets are off—you'll be fighting to stay awake longer than them!) This doesn't mean that you have to have your day scheduled in fifteen-minute increments, but some predictable patterns in the morning and evening can go a long way. Adding family rituals, such as Taco Tuesday or Fun-Night Friday (when you watch movies or play games together), is another way to maintain some predictability and connection as a family. Children will realize that there is family time, and then there are times when their parents prioritize each other (e.g., Saturday is date night), and they come to learn this over time. By incorporating structure and predictability in the form of routines, rituals, and traditions, you are also strengthening your marriage or long-term relationship by creating opportunities for shared experiences as a couple with your children. In addition, routines can make for more content children, which makes for less stressed parents and, therefore, a less stressed marriage.

3. Set boundaries with your children. As much as we want to give our children the world, having boundaries and saying no is healthy. Kids who have fewer limits and boundaries tend to have more behavioral issues. Children need to know that they are safe and loved, and we want to provide reassurance that both of those things are true, but that does not mean your children are the boss. You are. Conflict in marriage can arise if one parent feels he or she is constantly undermined by the other—one parent is the limit setter while the other allows the children to call the shots. By setting boundaries with your children and the expectation that you and your partner both are the parents, you can not only help prevent or quell behavioral issues but also make sure that the two of you are on the same page when it comes to setting limits.

4. Explore your parenting styles. Talk with each other about how each of you was raised. Often, we parent the way we were parented. Or the

reverse is true—we vow to never raise our kids the way we were raised. In either case, our pasts influence our present parenting—knowingly or not. Ask each other, when you reflect back on how you were parented, what you would keep and want to pass on through your own parenting to your children, and what you would get rid of. Couples may choose to write or journal about this subject on their own and then share their reflections. By having an understanding of each other's parenting styles or preferences—and how those came to be—you can make a better parenting team together.

5. Know that you and your partner do not need to parent exactly the same way. Yes, being a unified team when it comes to parenting is essential—however, it is natural for one of you to be more of the nurturer, while one tends to be more of the disciplinarian. It's natural for one of you to be more of the parent who plays, while the other prefers to do other activities with your children. Just as they will have different teachers in life, and different bosses, children benefit from multiple parenting approaches. Research on parenting styles has shown that there are three major types of parenting styles: authoritative, authoritarian, and permissive. Authoritative parenting tends to result in the most well-adjusted children with the fewest behavioral problems, better academic performance, and higher-quality relationships. This type of style is one in which you have high expectations of your children but you are also able to support them and allow them to express their feelings. Authoritarian is when parents have a strict approach, are highly demanding, are rigid about rules, and lack warmth and support. Authoritarian parenting often emphasizes punishment to teach children lessons. On the other end of the continuum is permissive parenting, in which parents provide a warm and loving environment but very little structure, do not enforce rules or expectations, and indulge all their children's wants and needs. Research has shown that children raised by authoritarian or permissive parents tend to struggle more socially, academically, or behaviorally. We advise that parents work toward a more authoritative style. Even if within that there are parenting differences or disagreements, you're likely to have better-adjusted children and a happier home. Parenting styles can be hard to adjust, so we would suggest working with a parenting coach or family

therapist if you're having a hard time. If you and your partner can agree to work toward a more authoritative style *together*, your chances of having better-adjusted children—and less conflict about how to parent them—are much higher.

6. Don't forget to talk about your parenting expectations. As we mentioned, often it's the expectations we have that are causing the issue. In order to talk about these, you and your partner can have an intentional, focused conversation during which you lay out all the expectations you have for each other as parents and expectations you have regarding the children. Expectations will change as children get older. Infants require a different form of childcare (e.g., who will do the feeding, get up with the baby, change diapers) from preteens or adolescents (e.g., who will have the conversation about puberty and sex, who will register them for extracurricular activities). For parents with newborns and toddlers, laying out expectations and negotiating these is critical because it's a stage in which you are both exhausted and tensions can run high simply because you're tired, and the emotional adjustment of a new baby is wildly underemphasized and can smack parents in the face if they aren't prepared. Having these conversations ahead of time and deciding on a plan together can greatly benefit your relationship by cutting off potential disagreements in their path and strengthening your communication and connection.

7. Parenting success relies more on the repair of parenting mistakes than parenting perfection. Think you have to be a near-perfect parent in order to have healthy, well-adjusted kids? Think again! Literature on children and attachment has shown that we actually need to get it right only about 30 percent of the time with our children.[3] It's more about how you come back together when you get off track—it's how you do that repair. Repair can happen when you acknowledge that you made a mistake and offer a sincere apology. For example, you could say, "I'm sorry I yelled at you. I was feeling frustrated and Mommy lost her temper, and that probably made you feel pretty lousy." This includes an apology in which you take ownership, express your feeling and behavior, and then acknowledge the impact on how it made your child feel. Repair can also happen by prioritizing connection after a period of disconnection. One way to do that is to have "special time in" when,

at the same time every day, you spend ten minutes with zero distractions doing an activity that your child chooses—giving your child one-on-one, undivided attention. Knowing that the repair matters, you are more likely to support your spouse when he or she screws up and praise him or her for the repair (e.g., saying "I'm sorry"). Further, you can model this practice in your own relationship with your partner by admitting when you're wrong, acknowledging how your spouse or partner may have felt, and saying that you are sorry. By practicing "special time in," you will also have an opportunity to have dedicated time with each child. This process can cut down on the resentment that sometimes happens in marriages when one parent feels like he or she doesn't get to spend as much time with the children because he or she is too busy around the house or too busy working, or if the spouse feels like he or she is always the disciplinarian.

Tom and Mariana: Mild Relationship Symptoms Related to Children and Parenting

Tom and Mariana have had some disagreements about household responsibilities, with Mariana feeling like she carries the majority of the load in the family, including child-rearing. Tom thinks that Mariana is too strict with their children; Mariana believes Tom could put his foot down so that she's not always the bad guy. They often find themselves on different pages when it comes to their parenting, and it is confusing the kids while also causing resentment and conflict in the marriage. Tom and Mariana were raised quite differently. Mariana, of Colombian descent, was raised by her mother and grandmother, who demanded much from her. Her brothers were treated like kings in the house, and she often felt that her brothers were spoiled while she had to overachieve in every way, from her housework to her schoolwork, and she worked at their family restaurant at a young age. She believes that the high demands on her led to her success. Tom, also raised by a single mother, grew up in a home where he didn't have a lot of rules—his mother worked two jobs, so he was left to fend for himself. He recalls his childhood being happy but says that "I came and went as I pleased and I turned out fine." Tom believes kids should "be kids" and prioritizes their playtime and playdates. Mariana, by contrast, believes that children should be taught the value of a dollar at an early age and that they need to help out around the house and do their part. Tom feels like Mariana is too harsh with the children, saying, "Not everything has to be about teaching them a lesson." Mariana believes Tom is "too soft on the kids—they will never learn right and wrong unless he steps up." Mariana and Tom both work and juggle child-rearing, but Mariana (like many mothers) feels like she does the majority of the work in the home and the work related to their kids. She complains, "He comes home and it's all fun and games," and secretly says, "I wish I could be the fun parent—they seem to enjoy him more than me." Tom says, "She just wants to put our kids to work like she had to growing up," while "I want them to play, and kids should be able to just be kids."

Keanu and Kate: Moderate Relationship Symptoms Related to Children and Parenting

Keanu and Kate are a couple who have a great deal of love, respect, and admiration for each other. Prior to having kids, they were a solid team and did everything together. They were one of those couples other couples were jealous of—like, do they really spend all their time together? Their first child, Marky, was an easygoing boy whom they could take anywhere. Max was born five years after Marky after they struggled to conceive, ultimately turning to in vitro fertilization (IVF) to have Max. Max has a more difficult temperament and was born at the beginning of the pandemic and never had an opportunity to separate from them. Kate, who had struggled for so long to get pregnant, had significant postpartum anxiety and was preoccupied with something bad happening to her baby; she didn't want to let him out of her sight, and the pandemic did not help matters, as it compounded her anxiety. Max was with Kate 24/7, minus brief breaks in which he would go with Keanu only if Keanu carried him around. Keanu said, "I can't put him down or he screams," and "His screams go right through you—I can't ignore them!" If Max wasn't being held by his parents or having a treat, he would have intense tantrums that lasted until Keanu or Kate gave in to his demands to either carry him or give him a popsicle. He refused to sleep in his own bed, so Kate slept with Max while Keanu slept in the room with Marky. Keanu and Kate went to bed when the kids were tired and fell asleep. Not only had they not slept in their bed together since Max was born, but they also had not had a date night since her pregnancy with him—it had been over two and a half years. Kate has been miserable for the last two years—she loves being a mother but says, "I don't know what my purpose is," and "I'm just Max and Marky's mom." Keanu, frustrated by seeing his wife so unhappy and feeling disconnected from her, misses his wife but is so overwhelmed by Max's demands that he can't think straight. Marky, who is usually so easy-going, has made statements to his grandparents that "Mommy loves Maxy more than me." Keanu and Kate, although well-intentioned, loving parents, have essentially created a tiny little monster who has been the baby boss of the entire family—and they have significantly neglected each other and their relationship. If they aren't careful, they could unintentionally destroy their marriage, which has been eroding with the passing months.

Brett and Tabitha: Severe Relationship Symptoms Related to Children and Parenting

Unfortunately, Brett and Tabitha's fights have been escalating—over bills, how they spend their time, the children, and whether they should separate. Not fighting fairly, they have been pulling the children into their arguments and drawing battle lines, with the kids taking sides. Even worse, Brett and Tabitha both seem to be undermining the other's relationship with the children. Each of them has been confiding in their children about their complaints related to the other. Brett has been telling the kids that their mother is spending all their money, while Tabitha has been saying Brett is no fun and won't let them go on a vacation or let the kids go to camps. There have been many evenings when they are fighting and the kids, although they retreat to their rooms, are often trying to sleep over loud yelling. Their oldest child, Danny, recently has been coming out of his room and trying to intervene between them. All three children are struggling in school, and the younger two children are showing signs of depression. Brett and Tabitha both grew up in homes where their parents struggled with addiction or depression—their parents were either harsh and punitive or simply not available. Both sets of parents separated or divorced, and they each were pulled into the high conflicts between their parents in a way that impacted their well-being.

RELATIONSHIP Rx FOR EACH COUPLE

Couple: Tom and Mariana

Prescription: Relationship Vitamins: Parenting Book Club;
Intentional Conversation about Expectations; Daily Kiss

Parenting Book Club

Tom and Mariana would benefit from increasing their understanding that children benefit from different parenting approaches. A trip to the library might help them with this task. Tom and Mariana had a common dynamic that many parents do—not communicating about parenting expectations and having different expectations of what it means to parent effectively. Tom and Mariana were actually both right. Tom was correct in that children need play and playdates in order to develop and meet certain milestones. Play is essentially the major "job" that young children and school-age children have. It has a number of positive effects in the brain, such as increasing the size of the prefrontal cortex—the area that helps with problem-solving, planning, and regulating emotions. Kids need other kids; socialization is one of the major ways children learn how to be and act in the world. At the same time, Mariana was right. Research suggests that giving children as young as three chores around the house actually improves their self-esteem and level of responsibility and increases their ability to handle frustration and adversity.[4] Children can be given developmentally appropriate tasks, such as putting their clothes in their hampers, making their beds, doing dishes, setting the table, feeding the dog, or helping out with cooking or laundry. In addition to helping them feel like contributing members of the family, giving them tasks they can do helps set the foundation for functioning independently and gives them opportunities for success. There are several parenting books available on general parenting, discipline, the importance of play, and how to involve children in helping around the house. Tom and Mariana could benefit from reading some parenting books together (or listening to audiobooks or podcasts) and talking about what they liked and didn't like and why.

Intentional Conversation about Expectations

Tom and Mariana would benefit from talking about how they were parented and using the strategy we recommend earlier in this chapter about what they would want to keep from how they were raised and what they would get rid of. After a few weeks of having their parenting book club, similar to talking through household responsibilities (see chapter 8), Tom and Mariana could list all the tasks of parenting, discuss their expectations for each of these, and assign roles.

Examples on this list could include the following:

- Knowing where the children are at any given time
- Finding childcare—babysitters, nannies, or day care settings
- Making and tracking medical and dental appointments
- Taking kids to the dentist or doctor
- Putting the children to bed
- Getting the kids up and going in the morning
- Monitoring toothbrushing and bathing
- Overseeing chores
- Planning birthday parties
- Buying gifts for friends' birthdays and holidays
- Transporting the children to extracurricular activities, sports, or playdates
- Assisting with homework
- Staying in touch with teachers or day care

Daily Kiss

This is a must-do assignment for all parents, and it takes only thirty seconds or less of your time. Prioritize kissing your spouse, passionately, for five to thirty seconds. This act helps you connect to each other in a way that is more than just "Mommy and Daddy" and signals that you are partners and lovers too. This doesn't mean that you'll end up between the sheets after that kiss, but it's a good way to set the tone that your marriage takes priority. Try it for two weeks and then tell us it wasn't effective—we bet you won't.

Couple: Keanu and Kate

Prescription: Relationship Medicine: "We Come First"; Reinstate Date Night; Extinguish Bad Behavior

"We Come First": Prioritize Time as a Couple and Attack the Problem, Not Each Other

The strategy of "We Come First" means that you and your partner prioritize time as a couple while you also identify what the problem is and attack the problem, not each other. Keanu and Kate realized that they had a couple of major issues happening—loss of control and upside-down boundaries, less time for them to connect, and disrupted sleep. The child was calling all the shots and had so much tiny-person power that the adults were actually sleeping in separate beds. Max had them trained to give him whatever he wanted as long as he cried loud enough or long enough.

First, they needed to prioritize the marital bed and stop the separate-bed fiasco. This was Mommy and Daddy's bed, period. That's not to say they wouldn't have nights or early mornings when the kids ended up in there, but first they needed to make a boundary around their relationship and allow for more time with each other, including physical contact. Doing so also helped better protect their sleep—which was critical for their physical and mental health—and better sleep meant better parents. Prioritizing your marriage will not hurt your kids. Hear us on this while we yell it at you: *Prioritizing your relationship is good for your children!* Full stop.

Reinstate Date Night

As you could probably predict right now, we were suggesting that Keanu and Kate immediately reinstate date night—at least three times per month and ideally weekly. They could ask family members or close friends to watch the kids, starting at their home at first and eventually building up to staying overnight at Grandma's house.

The date night would do a few things: give them time to connect, just the two of them; allow Kate to feel like a real person, wife, and woman again and not just "Max and Marky's mom"; and allow their kids to connect with others and help Max realize that he could separate from his parents and they would come back. Like all children, Max had to figure out his two-year-old business, and, unfortunately like many COVID-19 babies, he hadn't learned how to fully soothe himself, a task that is critical to development. Each parent, especially Kate, would need to be reminded that Max separating from them for small periods of time (and her separating from him) was good for Max—and good for their whole family.

Extinguish Bad Behavior

Keanu and Kate aren't alone in this dynamic in which children end up calling the shots or the universe revolves around the kids. However, they had empowered two-year-old Max in a way that wasn't good for their marriage (and actually wasn't good for Max either). Keanu and Kate needed to address the bad behavior that was happening—on their part and on Max's—and work as a team to put a stop to it. This challenging task would require them to lean on each other, and trust the process, in order to extinguish Max's tantrums through active ignoring and not giving in to him. They would need to come up with a plan, in advance (not in the moment because when your child is screaming you can't think straight—that's just biology), about what their approach would be. Given that Max engaged in tantrums that could last over an hour, it wouldn't make sense to do a titrated approach (like baby steps). When Max asked to be picked up or for another popsicle, both parents would firmly say no. And then, no matter what, they had to stick to that answer. If Max threw a tantrum, he could do so in his room, away from the other family members. This was not to punish Max; rather, it would allow Max to see that he could calm himself down (eventually), avoid any unintentional attention (called "negative reinforcement") that his parents or brother might give him during said tantrum, and save the eardrums of his parents. This would likely be difficult for Keanu and Kate and might take several days or a couple weeks. We often advise parents to either get a good set of earplugs or take turns being in the house so one parent can go outside to catch his or her breath. If they are not able to do this on their own, we strongly advise talking with their pediatrician or working with a parenting coach or family therapist skilled in behavioral modification in children.

Couple: Brett and Tabitha

Prescription: Relationship CPR: Couples Therapy and the Children Are Off-Limits

Brett and Tabitha could benefit from working with a couples therapist on a whole host of issues. Prior to doing so, they needed to establish ground rules that the children were off-limits. No more pulling them into arguments and no more talking about the other parent in a negative way to the children.

Nobody has children and says, "I'm going to be the worst parent I can possibly be." Parents want to protect their kids by having them wear seat belts and bike helmets, by having them eat healthy food, and by taking them to the doctor and giving them medicine when they are sick. What happens sometimes is that couples can get so caught up in their marital conflicts, they don't see those conflicts as toxins—invisible viruses that are infecting their children. That is exactly what had happened with Brett and Tabitha—they were so caught up in their anger toward the other that they didn't see the impact this problem had been having on their children.

Tabitha had admitted that there were times when she hated Brett, but she should ask herself in those moments, did she hate her husband more than she loved her children? The answer to that should be pretty easy. The children needed to be extracted from the war between the parents. Not only was it lousy parenting in the short term, and enormously stressful for the kids, but it would also have long-term consequences for their children into adulthood.

In couples therapy, they could address the layers of conflict between them and prioritize their roles as parents. It might be that they did decide to go the route of separation. In therapy, they could talk through co-parenting and how they might help their children through that painful process. Or they could make major strides and return to a happier time in their marriage and know that they prioritized each other and their children's well-being by seeking help and quitting their bad behavior concerning the kids.

Summary

Parenting is not easy, nor are we trying to say that it is. Parenting is also an arena in which there are so many potential conflicts that can cause minor squabbles (if not all-out catastrophic battles) in marriages. In order to re-solve disagreements that will inevitably arise when it comes to kids, parents can prepare by having intentional conversations, doing their homework, and discussing parenting roles. Being aware of how our own parenting past (how we were raised) affects our parenting present can give good insight into what we value from our own childhood and what we'd rather do away with when it comes to our children. Most important, in addition to providing love and structure for kids, the best thing couples can do for their children is love each other and prioritize their relationship over everything else. By being on similar pages of the parenting playbook (it doesn't even have to be the exact same page!), we will drastically cut down on any potential resentment, annoyance, or irritation with our spouses and inevitably create stronger connections with our partners in which we each feel supported by the other doing the hardest but most rewarding job we'll ever have to do, together.

CONCLUSION

Nobody said relationships were easy. If someone told you that, they were lying to you. Relationship experts will tell you that you have to put in "the work" in order to achieve the marital or relationship satisfaction and happiness that you want. What experts don't always tell you is that you don't have to work with a couples therapist when you're at your wits' end in order to achieve relationship success. In fact, with some simple tools and strategies, just like taking your daily vitamins, you can prevent relationship problems and improve the overall "immune system" of your relationship, protecting it from stressors or other harmful invaders. Further, if your relationship has become less than healthy, there are more intensive strategies that can be employed—just like taking medication for an illness. If your marriage or relationship is at death's door, there are tools and strategies that can be utilized to resuscitate a dying relationship.

We are professionals who work with couples every single day in a number of different capacities. Don't get us wrong; we are huge supporters of couples therapy and do a tremendous amount of couples work—*and* we know that you don't have to go to a couples therapist to try some things that can actually be therapeutic for your relationship. Our hope is that this book will give *all* couples the tools they need in the form of Relationship Vitamins and Medicine to avoid ever having to do something as drastic as intensive marriage counseling, hiring divorce lawyers, or (gasp!) going on a reality TV show to save their marriages.

Throughout this book, we have presented numerous couples—many just like you—who struggle with some of the most common issues in relationships: trust, emotional and sexual intimacy, unmet expectations, fear of change, money, children, friends-and-family drama, and other topics. All our couples have benefited from various degrees of intervention—strategies that are grounded in relationship science—from Relationship Vitamins to Relationship Medicine to even, for some, Relationship CPR.

Even if Prince Charming wed Cinderella, there is no relationship that is immune to difficulties or problems over time. Outside influences, like viruses, in the form of contempt, toxic family members, financial disputes, or trust issues, can infect a reasonably healthy relationship over time without the right tools or supports in place to prevent that from happening. In this book, we have grounded our advice and strategies in relationship science, including evidence-based approaches that consider attachment styles, healthy versus toxic communication, and complex family-system dynamics.

In this book, you have seen that research on attachment styles has dramatically shifted the way we approach couples work. Just by having an increased understanding of what your attachment style (and that of your partner) may be, you can drastically improve your understanding of each other—an explanation (though not an excuse) for why your partner does or says the things that he or she does. Although we cannot go into detail about each of our couples' individual attachment styles, much of their behavior with each other is heavily influenced by this template—we bring our attachment styles in our invisible suitcases into our relationships. Unpacking those suitcases and understanding our partners' pasts, as well as how we learned to attach to others and how it influences our other relationships, can be a relationship game changer.

We talk—a lot—about talking in this book. Healthy communication is one of the best thermometers for a healthy relationship. Couples who are respectfully able to sit with each other, even if conversations are difficult, and talk things through in a way that's *goal-directed*, in which it is *you and me against the problem* instead of *you and me against each other*, have a much better prognosis. When it comes to communication, we want to emphasize that *it is just as much about being heard and understood by a partner* as it is about the content of the communication itself. If communication is lacking or is unhealthy, there are simple tools you can utilize, which we have highlighted in many of our Relationship Vitamins and Medicine exercises.

Speaking of communication, we caution you to pay attention to where contempt may have entered your relationship—or to know what contempt is so you can stop it in its infectious and dangerous tracks. Contempt is a major predictor of divorce, so if you recognize it—such as when one partner points out that there is a critical flaw in the other, while elevating himself or herself, in a way to shame the other or make the other feel less than worthy—it's time to start working on some exercises to stop it. Instead of focusing on the negative and unhealthy communication, one of the biggest takeaways we want to make sure you remember is to never stop appreciating your partner. Praise and reinforcement aren't just for dog training or teaching preschoolers to stay on task—these practices are just as important in adulthood and in our romantic relationships. Yet, over time, appreciation is often one of the first things to go, which results in spouses feeling taken for granted and resentful. Never stop praising or thanking or complimenting your partner—or reminding yourself that nobody is perfect. Your partner has so many positive qualities that drew you to him or her in the first place—and so many more that you've identified since then—and he or she needs to hear this from you.

Lastly, we hope that this book brings some hope to you—knowing that there are things you can do to strengthen your relationship, shore up your relationship "immunity," and even bring a struggling marriage back to health. There is no relationship that is immune to problems—but just like you can take care of your body in the form of exercises and vitamins, there are strategies you can use to effect change and improve your relationship in ways you never thought possible.

NOTES

CHAPTER 1. FEAR OF CHANGE

1. K. H. Blanchard, P. Zigarmi, and D. Zigarmi, *Leadership and the One Minute Manager: Increasing Effectiveness through Situational Leadership* (New York: William Morrow, 1996).

2. H. Boschi, *Why We Do What We Do: Understanding Our Brain to Get the Best Out of Ourselves and Others* (Hoboken: John Wiley & Sons, 2020).

3. A. de Berker et al., "Computations of Uncertainty Mediate Acute Stress Responses in Humans," *Nature Communications* 7, 10996 (2016).

4. "Love Builder: Our Training," Love Builder, accessed April 5, 2022, https://lovebuilder.com/our-training.

CHAPTER 2. TRUST: YOUR PAST IS INTERFERING WITH YOUR PRESENT

1. Cindy Hazan and Phillip R. Shaver, "Attachment as an Organizational Framework for Research on Close Relationships," *Psychological Inquiry* 5 (1994): 1–22.

2. Lee A. Kirkpatrick and Cindy Hazan, "Attachment Styles and Close Relationships: A Four-Year Prospective Study," *Personal Relationships* 1, no. 2 (1994): 123–42.

3. Lindsey M. Rodriguez et al., "The Price of Distrust: Trust, Anxious Attachment, Jealousy, and Partner Abuse," *Partner Abuse* 6, no. 3 (2015): 298–319.

4. James A. Coan, Hillary S. Schaefer, and Richard J. Davidson, "Lending a Hand: Social Regulation of the Neural Response to Threat," *Psychological Science*

17, no. 12 (December 2006): 1032–39; Brooke C. Feeney, "A Secure Base: Responsive Support of Goal Strivings and Exploration in Adult Intimate Relationships," *Journal of Personality and Social Psychology* 87, no. 5 (2004): 631; Brooke C. Feeney and Roxanne L. Thrush, "Relationship Influences on Exploration in Adulthood: The Characteristics and Function of a Secure Base," *Journal of Personality and Social Psychology* 98, no. 1 (2010): 57; Brian Baker et al., "Marital Support, Spousal Contact and the Course of Mild Hypertension," *Journal of Psychosomatic Research* 55, no. 3 (2003): 229–33.

5. Jack P. Shonkoff et al., "The Lifelong Effects of Early Childhood Adversity and Toxic Stress," *Pediatrics* 129, no. 1 (2012): e232–e246; Hillary A. Franke, "Toxic Stress: Effects, Prevention and Treatment," *Children* 1, no. 3 (2014): 390–402; Jeffry A. Simpson and W. Steven Rholes, "Adult Attachment, Stress, and Romantic Relationships," *Current Opinion in Psychology* 13 (2017): 19–24.

6. Katrijn Brenning et al., "An Adaptation of the Experiences in Close Relationships Scale–Revised for Use with Children and Adolescents," *Journal of Social and Personal Relationships* 28, no. 8 (2011): 1048–72.

7. Amir Levine and Rachel Heller, *Attached: The New Science of Adult Attachment and How It Can Help You Find—and Keep—Love* (New York: Penguin Random House, 2010).

CHAPTER 3. LACK OF EMOTIONAL INTIMACY

1. Helen Fisher et al., "Romantic Love: An fMRI Study of a Neural Mechanism for Mate Choice," *Journal of Comparative Neurology* 493, no. 1 (2005): 58–62; Bianca P. Acevedo et al., "Neural Correlates of Long-Term Intense Romantic Love," *Social Cognitive and Affective Neuroscience* 7, no. 2 (2012): 145–59.

2. John M. Gottman, *The Science of Trust: Emotional Attunement for Couples* (New York: W. W. Norton, 2011).

CHAPTER 4. LOSS OF SEXUAL INTIMACY AND ATTRACTION

1. Helen Fisher, *Anatomy of Love: A Natural History of Mating, Marriage, and Why We Stray*, 2nd edition (New York: W. W. Norton, 2016).

2. Georgia Stathopoulou, Mark B. Powers, Angela C. Berry, Jasper A. J. Smits, and Michael W. Otto, "Exercise Interventions for Mental Health: A Quantitative and Qualitative Review," *Clinical Psychology: Science and Practice* 13, no. 2 (2006): 179; Lynette L. Craft and Frank M. Perna, "The Benefits of Exercise for the Clini-

cally Depressed," *Primary Care Companion to the Journal of Clinical Psychiatry* 6, no. 3 (2004): 104; Felipe B. Schuch, Davy Vancampfort, Justin Richards, Simon Rosenbaum, Philip B. Ward, and Brendon Stubbs, "Exercise as a Treatment for Depression: A Meta-Analysis Adjusting for Publication Bias," *Journal of Psychiatric Research* 77 (2016): 42–51.

3. Nicholas Wolfinger, "Does Sexual History Affect Marital Happiness?" Institute for Family Studies, 2018, https://ifstudies.org/blog/does-sexual-history-affect -marital-happiness.

4. T. J. Starks et al., "The Prevalence and Correlates of Sexual Arrangements in a National Cohort of HIV-Negative Gay and Bisexual Men in the United States," *Archives of Sexual Behavior* 48, no. 1 (2019): 369–82, https://doi.org/10.1007 /s10508-018-1282-8; E. C. Levine et al., "Open Relationships, Nonconsensual Nonmonogamy, and Monogamy among U.S. Adults: Findings from the 2012 National Survey of Sexual Health and Behavior," *Archives of Sexual Behavior* 47, no. 5 (2018): 1439–50, https://doi.org/10.1007/s10508-018-1178-7.

CHAPTER 5. UNMET EXPECTATIONS AND UNFULFILLED NEEDS

1. Norval D. Glenn, *With This Ring: A National Survey on Marriage in America* (Washington, DC: National Fatherhood Initiative, 2005): 1–38.

2. Donald H. Baucom et al., "The Role of Cognitions in Marital Relationships: Definitional, Methodological, and Conceptual Issues," *Journal of Consulting and Clinical Psychology* 57, no. 1 (1989): 31; John Mordechai Gottman and Julie Schwartz Gottman, "Gottman Method Couple Therapy," *Clinical Handbook of Couple Therapy* 4, no. 8 (2008): 138–64.

3. John Mordechai Gottman and Julie Schwartz Gottman, "Gottman Method Couple Therapy," *Clinical Handbook of Couple Therapy* 4, no. 8 (2008): 138–64.

4. Janice Driver, Amber Tabares, Alyson F. Shapiro, and John M. Gottman, "Couple Interaction in Happy and Unhappy Marriages: Gottman Laboratory Studies," in *Normal Family Processes: Growing Diversity and Complexity*, edited by F. Walsh (New York: Guilford Press, 2012), 57–77.

CHAPTER 7. DISRESPECT AND CONTEMPT

1. J. M. Gottman, *What Predicts Divorce?* (Hillsdale: Lawrence Erlbaum, 1994).

2. Gottman, *What Predicts Divorce?*

3. J. M. Gottman, *Why Marriages Succeed or Fail* (New York: Simon and Schuster, 1994); J. M. Gottman and R. W. Levenson, "Marital Processes Predictive of Later Dissolution: Behavior, Physiology, and Health," *Journal of Personality and Social Psychology* 63, no. 2 (1992): 221–33.

4. Claudia M. Gold and Ed Tronick, *The Power of Discord: Why the Ups and Downs of Relationships Are the Secret to Building Intimacy, Resilience, and Trust* (New York: Little, Brown Spark, 2020).

5. John Mordechai Gottman and Robert Wayne Levenson, "What Predicts Change in Marital Interaction over Time? A Study of Alternative Models," *Family Process* 38, no. 2 (1999): 143–58.

CHAPTER 8. HOUSEHOLD RESPONSIBILITIES

1. Daniel L. Carlson et al., "The Gendered Division of Housework and Couples' Sexual Relationships: A Reexamination," *Journal of Marriage and Family* 78, no. 4 (2016): 975–95; "Modern Marriage," Pew Research Center's Social and Demographic Trends Project, Pew Research Center, accessed May 30, 2020, https://www.pewresearch.org/social-trends/2007/07/18/modern-marriage/.

2. Matthew D. Johnson, Nancy L. Galambos, and Jared R. Anderson, "Skip the Dishes? Not So Fast! Sex and Housework Revisited," *Journal of Family Psychology* 30, no. 2 (2016): 203–13, https://doi.org/10.1037/fam0000161.

3. Mylène Lachance-Grzela and Geneviève Bouchard, "Why Do Women Do the Lion's Share of Housework? A Decade of Research," *Sex Roles* 63, no. 11 (2010): 767–80; Melanie E. Brewster, "Lesbian Women and Household Labor Division: A Systematic Review of Scholarly Research from 2000 to 2015," *Journal of Lesbian Studies* 21, no. 1 (2017): 47–69, https://doi.org/10.1080/10894160.2016.1142350; S. L. Tornello, B. N. Sonnenberg, and C. J. Patterson, "Division of Labor among Gay Fathers: Associations with Parent, Couple, and Child Adjustment," *Psychology of Sexual Orientation and Gender Diversity* 2, no. 4 (2015): 365–75, https://doi.org/10.1037/sgd0000109.

4. Abbie E. Goldberg, JuliAnna Z. Smith, and Maureen Perry-Jenkins, "The Division of Labor in Lesbian, Gay, and Heterosexual New Adoptive Parents," *Journal of Marriage and Family* 74, no. 4 (2012): 812–28, http://www.jstor.org/stable/41678757.

5. Javier Cerrato and Eva Cifre, "Gender Inequality in Household Chores and Work-Family Conflict," *Frontiers in Psychology* 9, 1330 (August 3, 2018), https://doi.org/10.3389/fpsyg.2018.01330; "Parenting in America," Pew Research Cen-

ter, December 17, 2015, https://www.pewresearch.org/social-trends/2015/12/17/parenting-in-america/.

6. Daniel L. Carlson, Amanda J. Miller, and Stephanie Rudd, "Division of Housework, Communication, and Couples' Relationship Satisfaction," *Socius: Sociological Research for a Dynamic World* 6 (2020): 1–17, https://doi.org/10.1177/2378023120924805.

7. Paul Schrodt, Paul L. Witt, and Jenna R. Shimkowski, "A Meta-Analytical Review of the Demand/Withdraw Pattern of Interaction and Its Associations with Individual, Relational, and Communicative Outcomes," *Communication Monographs* 81, no. 1 (2014): 28–58.

8. Daniel L. Carlson, Amanda Jayne Miller, and Sharon Sassler, "Stalled for Whom? Change in the Division of Particular Housework Tasks and Their Consequences for Middle- to Low-Income Couples," *Socius* (January 2018), https://doi.org/10.1177/2378023118765867; Johnson et al., "Skip the Dishes? Not So Fast!"

9. R. M. Horne et al., "Time, Money, or Gender? Predictors of the Division of Household Labour Across Life Stages," *Sex Roles* 78 (2018): 731–43; Scott Coltrane, "Research on Household Labor: Modeling and Measuring the Social Embeddedness of Routine Family Work," *Journal of Marriage and Family* 62, no. 4 (2000): 1208–33; Johnson et al., "Skip the Dishes? Not So Fast!"

10. "CCF BRIEF: Not All Housework Is Created Equal: Particular Housework Tasks and Couples' Relationship Quality," Council on Contemporary Families, n.d., https://sites.utexas.edu/contemporaryfamilies/2018/04/03/houseworkandrelationshipquality/; Carlson et al., "Stalled for Whom?"

11. Carlson et al., "Stalled for Whom?"

CHAPTER 9. MONEY AND FINANCES

1. Rachel Cruze and Ramsey Solutions, "Money, Marriage, and Communication," *Ramsey Solutions*, accessed December 2021, https://cdn.ramseysolutions.net/media/b2c/personalities/rachel/PR/MoneyMarriageAndCommunication.pdf?_ga=2.229342364.1459077490.1529939751-931704233.1526573748&_gac=1.40038166.1526574640.EAIaIQobChMIxN3Xq5WN2wIVjeDICh1UAwVjEAAYASAAEgIvT_D_BwE.

2. "POLL: How Husbands and Wives Really Feel about Their Finances," *Money*, accessed June 2022, https://money.com/love-money-by-the-numbers/.

3. Michelle M. Jeanfreau, Kenji Noguchi, Michael D. Mong, and Hans Stadthagen-Gonzalez, "Financial Infidelity in Couple Relationships," *Journal of Financial Therapy* 9, no. 1 (2018): 1.

4. Jessica Griffin and Jonathan Francetic, "Love Builder Online Relationship Course—The Home Office: Finances, Career and Life Planning," Love Builder, 2019, https://www.lovebuilder.com.

CHAPTER 10. FRIENDS AND FAMILY

1. S. Cohen et al., "Social Ties and Susceptibility to the Common Cold," *JAMA* 277, no. 24 (1997): 1940–44; Kara Takasaki, "Friends and Family in Relationship Communities: The Importance of Friendship during the Transition to Adulthood," *Michigan Family Review* 1 (2017): 76–96; Kirsten Voss, Dorothy Markiewicz, and Anna Beth Doyle, "Friendship, Marriage and Self-Esteem," *Journal of Social and Personal Relationships* 16, no. 1 (February 1999): 103–22, https://doi.org/10.1177/0265407599161006; Julianne Holt-Lunstad et al., "Loneliness and Social Isolation as Risk Factors for Mortality: A Meta-Analytic Review," *Perspectives on Psychological Science* 10, no. 2 (March 2015): 227–37, https://doi.org/10.1177/1745691614568352.

2. "Building Your Resilience," American Psychological Association, updated February 1, 2020, https://www.apa.org/topics/resilience.

3. Esther Perel, *Mating in Captivity: Reconciling the Erotic and the Domestic* (New York: HarperCollins, 2006).

CHAPTER 11. CHILDREN AND PARENTING

1. Renee Stepler, "Led by Baby Boomers, Divorce Rates Climb for America's 50+ Population," Pew Research Center, published March 9, 2017, https://www.pewresearch.org/fact-tank/2017/03/09/led-by-baby-boomers-divorce-rates-climb-for-americas-50-population/; Susan L. Brown and I-Fen Lin, "The Gray Divorce Revolution: Rising Divorce among Middle-Aged and Older Adults, 1990–2010," *The Journals of Gerontology: Series B* 67, no. 6 (2012): 731–41.

2. Heather C. Forkey, Jessica L. Griffin, and Moira Szilagyi, *Childhood Trauma and Resilience* (Itasca: American Academy of Pediatrics, 2021).

3. Claudia M. Gold and Ed Tronick, *The Power of Discord: Why the Ups and Downs of Relationships Are the Secret to Building Intimacy, Resilience, and Trust* (New York: Little, Brown Spark, 2020), 36–39.

4. George E. Vaillant, Charles C. McArthur, and Arlie Bock, "Grant Study of Adult Development, 1938–2000," *Harvard Dataverse* V4 (2010), https://doi.org/10.7910/DVN/48WRX9.

BIBLIOGRAPHY

Acevedo, Bianca P., Arthur Aron, Helen Fisher, and Lucy L. Brown. "Neural Correlates of Long-Term Intense Romantic Love." *Social Cognitive and Affective Neuroscience* 7, no. 2 (2012): 145–59.

Baker, Brian, John Paul Szalai, Miney Paquette, and Sheldon Tobe. "Marital Support, Spousal Contact and the Course of Mild Hypertension." *Journal of Psychosomatic Research* 55, no. 3 (2003): 229–33.

Baucom, Donald H., Norman Epstein, Steven L. Sayers, and Tamara G. Sher. "The Role of Cognitions in Marital Relationships: Definitional, Methodological, and Conceptual Issues." *Journal of Consulting and Clinical Psychology* 57, no. 1 (1989): 31.

Blanchard, Ken, Patricia Zigarmi, and Drea Zigarmi. *Leadership and the One Minute Manager: Increasing Effectiveness through Situational Leadership.* New York: William Morrow, 1996.

Boschi, Helena. *Why We Do What We Do: Understanding Our Brain to Get the Best Out of Ourselves and Others.* Hoboken, NJ: John Wiley & Sons, 2020.

Brenning, Katrijn, Bart Soenens, Caroline Braet, and Guy Bosmans. "An Adaptation of the Experiences in Close Relationships Scale–Revised for Use with Children and Adolescents." *Journal of Social and Personal Relationships* 28, no. 8 (2011): 1048–72.

Brewster, Melanie E. "Lesbian Women and Household Labor Division: A Systematic Review of Scholarly Research from 2000 to 2015." *Journal of Lesbian Studies* 21, no. 1 (2017): 47–69. https://doi.org/10.1080/10894160.2016.1142350.

Brown, Susan L., and I-Fen Lin. "The Gray Divorce Revolution: Rising Divorce among Middle-Aged and Older Adults, 1990–2010." *The Journals of Gerontology: Series B* 67, no. 6 (2012): 731–41.

"Building Your Resilience." American Psychological Association. Published January 1, 2012, updated February 1, 2020. https://www.apa.org/topics/resilience.

Carlson, Daniel L., Amanda J. Miller, and Stephanie Rudd. "Division of Housework, Communication, and Couples' Relationship Satisfaction." *Socius: Sociological Research for a Dynamic World* 6 (2020): 1–17. https://doi.org/10.1177/2378023120924805.

Carlson, Daniel L., Amanda J. Miller, Sharon Sassler, and Sarah Hanson. "The Gendered Division of Housework and Couples' Sexual Relationships: A Reexamination." *Journal of Marriage and Family* 78, no. 4 (2016): 975–95.

Carlson, Daniel L., Amanda Jayne Miller, and Sharon Sassler. "Stalled for Whom? Change in the Division of Particular Housework Tasks and Their Consequences for Middle- to Low-Income Couples." *Socius* (January 2018). https://doi.org/10.1177/2378023118765867.

"CCF BRIEF: Not All Housework Is Created Equal: Particular Housework Tasks and Couples' Relationship Quality." Council on Contemporary Families. n.d. https://sites.utexas.edu/contemporaryfamilies/2018/04/03/houseworkandrelationshipquality/.

Cerrato, Javier, and Eva Cifre. "Gender Inequality in Household Chores and Work-Family Conflict." *Frontiers in Psychology* 9, 1330 (August 3, 2018). https://doi.org/10.3389/fpsyg.2018.01330.

Coan, James A., Hillary S. Schaefer, and Richard J. Davidson. "Lending a Hand: Social Regulation of the Neural Response to Threat." *Psychological Science* 17, no. 12 (December 2006): 1032–39.

Cohen, S., W. J. Doyle, D. P. Skoner, B. S. Rabin, and J. M. Gwaltney Jr. "Social Ties and Susceptibility to the Common Cold." *JAMA* 277, no. 24 (1997): 1940–44.

Coltrane, Scott. "Research on Household Labor: Modeling and Measuring the Social Embeddedness of Routine Family Work." *Journal of Marriage and Family* 62, no. 4 (2000): 1208–33.

Craft, Lynette L., and Frank M. Perna. "The Benefits of Exercise for the Clinically Depressed." *Primary Care Companion to the Journal of Clinical Psychiatry* 6, no. 3 (2004): 104–11.

Cruze, Rachel, and Ramsey Solutions. "Money, Marriage, and Communication." *Ramsey Solutions.* Accessed December 2021. https://cdn.ramseysolutions.net/media/b2c/personalities/rachel/PR/MoneyMarriageAndCommunication.pdf?_ga=2.229342364.1459077490.1529939751-931704233.1526573748&

_gac=1.40038166.1526574640.EAIaIQobChMIxN3Xq5WN2wIVjeDICh1UA
wVjEAAYASAAEgIvT_D_BwE.

de Berker, Archy O., Robb B. Rutledge, Christoph Mathys, Louise Marshall, Gemma F. Cross, Raymond J. Dolan, and Sven Bestmann. "Computations of Uncertainty Mediate Acute Stress Responses in Humans." *Nature Communications* 7, 10996 (2016).

Driver, Janice, Amber Tabares, Alyson F. Shapiro, and John M. Gottman. "Couple Interaction in Happy and Unhappy Marriages: Gottman Laboratory Studies." In *Normal Family Processes: Growing Diversity and Complexity*, edited by F. Walsh, 57–77. New York: Guilford Press, 2012.

Feeney, Brooke C. "A Secure Base: Responsive Support of Goal Strivings and Exploration in Adult Intimate Relationships." *Journal of Personality and Social Psychology* 87, no. 5 (2004): 631.

Feeney, Brooke C., and Roxanne L. Thrush. "Relationship Influences on Exploration in Adulthood: The Characteristics and Function of a Secure Base." *Journal of Personality and Social Psychology* 98, no. 1 (2010): 57.

Fisher, Helen. *Anatomy of Love: A Natural History of Mating, Marriage, and Why We Stray*. 2nd edition. New York: W. W. Norton, 2016.

Fisher, Helen, Arthur Aron, and Lucy L. Brown. "Romantic Love: An fMRI Study of a Neural Mechanism for Mate Choice." *Journal of Comparative Neurology* 493, no. 1 (2005): 58–62.

Forkey, Heather C., Jessica L. Griffin, and Moira Szilagyi. *Childhood Trauma and Resilience*. Itasca: American Academy of Pediatrics, 2021.

Franke, Hillary A. "Toxic Stress: Effects, Prevention and Treatment." *Children* 1, no. 3 (2014): 390–402.

Glenn, Norval D. *With This Ring: A National Survey on Marriage in America*. Washington, DC: National Fatherhood Initiative, 2005.

Gold, Claudia M., and Ed Tronick. *The Power of Discord: Why the Ups and Downs of Relationships Are the Secret to Building Intimacy, Resilience, and Trust*. New York: Little, Brown Spark, 2020.

Goldberg, Abbie E., JuliAnna Z. Smith, and Maureen Perry-Jenkins. "The Division of Labor in Lesbian, Gay, and Heterosexual New Adoptive Parents." *Journal of Marriage and Family* 74, no. 4 (2012): 812–28. http://www.jstor.org/stable/41678757.

Gottman, John M. *The Science of Trust: Emotional Attunement for Couples*. New York: W. W. Norton, 2011.

Gottman, John M. *What Predicts Divorce? The Relationship between Marital Processes and Marital Outcomes*. Hillsdale: Lawrence Erlbaum, 1994.

Gottman, John M. *Why Marriages Succeed or Fail.* New York: Simon and Schuster, 1994.

Gottman, John M., and Robert W. Levenson. "Marital Processes Predictive of Later Dissolution: Behavior, Physiology, and Health." *Journal of Personality and Social Psychology* 63, no. 2 (1992): 221–33.

Gottman, John Mordechai, and Julie Schwartz Gottman. "Gottman Method Couple Therapy." *Clinical Handbook of Couple Therapy* 4, no. 8 (2008): 138–64.

Gottman, John Mordechai, and Robert Wayne Levenson. "What Predicts Change in Marital Interaction over Time? A Study of Alternative Models." *Family Process* 38, no. 2 (1999): 143–58.

Griffin, Jessica, and Jonathan Francetic. "Love Builder Online Relationship Course—The Home Office: Finances, Career and Life Planning." Love Builder. 2019. https://www.lovebuilder.com.

Hazan, Cindy, and Phillip R. Shaver. "Attachment as an Organizational Framework for Research on Close Relationships." *Psychological Inquiry* 5 (1994): 1–22.

Holt-Lunstad, Julianne, Timothy B. Smith, Mark Baker, Tyler Harris, and David Stephenson. "Loneliness and Social Isolation as Risk Factors for Mortality: A Meta-Analytic Review." *Perspectives on Psychological Science* 10, no. 2 (March 2015): 227–37. https://doi.org/10.1177/1745691614568352.

Horne, R. M., Matthew D. Johnson, Nancy L. Galambos, and Harvey J. Krahn. "Time, Money, or Gender? Predictors of the Division of Household Labour Across Life Stages." *Sex Roles* 78 (2018): 731–43.

Jeanfreau, Michelle M., Kenji Noguchi, Michael D. Mong, and Hans Stadthagen-Gonzalez. "Financial Infidelity in Couple Relationships." *Journal of Financial Therapy* 9, no. 1 (2018): 1.

Johnson, Matthew D., Nancy L. Galambos, and Jared R. Anderson. "Skip the Dishes? Not So Fast! Sex and Housework Revisited." *Journal of Family Psychology* 30, no. 2 (2016): 203–13. https://doi.org/10.1037/fam0000161.

Kirkpatrick, Lee A., and Cindy Hazan. "Attachment Styles and Close Relationships: A Four-Year Prospective Study." *Personal Relationships* 1, no. 2 (1994): 123–42.

Lachance-Grzela, Mylène, and Geneviève Bouchard. "Why Do Women Do the Lion's Share of Housework? A Decade of Research." *Sex Roles* 63, no. 11 (2010): 767–80.

Levine, Amir, and Rachel Heller. *Attached: The New Science of Adult Attachment and How It Can Help You Find—and Keep—Love.* New York: Penguin Random House, 2010.

Levine, Ethan Czuy, Debby Herbenick, Omar Martinez, Tsung-Chieh Fu, and Brian Dodge. "Open Relationships, Nonconsensual Nonmonogamy, and Monogamy among U.S. Adults: Findings from the 2012 National Survey of Sexual Health and Behavior." *Archives of Sexual Behavior* 47, no. 5 (2018): 1439–50. https://doi.org/10.1007/s10508-018-1178-7.

"Love Builder: Our Training." Love Builder. Accessed April 5, 2022. https://love builder.com/our-training.

"Modern Marriage." Pew Research Center's Social and Demographic Trends Project. Pew Research Center. Accessed May 30, 2020. https://www.pewresearch.org /social-trends/2007/07/18/modern-marriage/.

"Parenting in America." Pew Research Center, December 17, 2015. https://www .pewresearch.org/social-trends/2015/12/17/parenting-in-america/.

Perel, Esther. *Mating in Captivity: Reconciling the Erotic and the Domestic* (New York: HarperCollins, 2006).

"POLL: How Husbands and Wives Really Feel about Their Finances." *Money*. Accessed June 2022. https://money.com/love-money-by-the-numbers/.

Rodriguez, Lindsey M., Angelo M. DiBello, Camilla S. Overup, and Clayton Neighbors. "The Price of Distrust: Trust, Anxious Attachment, Jealousy, and Partner Abuse." *Partner Abuse* 6, no. 3 (2015): 298–319.

Schrodt, Paul, Paul L. Witt, and Jenna R. Shimkowski. "A Meta-Analytical Review of the Demand/Withdraw Pattern of Interaction and Its Associations with Individual, Relational, and Communicative Outcomes." *Communication Monographs* 81, no. 1 (2014): 28–58.

Schuch, Felipe B., Davy Vancampfort, Justin Richards, Simon Rosenbaum, Philip B. Ward, and Brendon Stubbs. "Exercise as a Treatment for Depression: A Meta-Analysis Adjusting for Publication Bias." *Journal of Psychiatric Research* 77 (2016): 42–51.

Shonkoff, Jack P., Andrew S. Garner, Benjamin S. Siegel, Mary I. Dobbins, Marian F. Earls, Laura McGuinn, John Pascoe, and David L. Wood. "The Lifelong Effects of Early Childhood Adversity and Toxic Stress." *Pediatrics* 129, no. 1 (2012): e232–e246.

Simpson, Jeffry A., and W. Steven Rholes. "Adult Attachment, Stress, and Romantic Relationships." *Current Opinion in Psychology* 13 (2017): 19–24.

Starks, Tyrel J., Gabriel Robles, Stephen C. Bosco, Trey V. Dellucci, Christian Grov, and Jeffrey T. Parsons. "The Prevalence and Correlates of Sexual Arrangements in a National Cohort of HIV-Negative Gay and Bisexual Men in the United States." *Archives of Sexual Behavior* 48, no. 1 (2019): 369–82. https://doi .org/10.1007/s10508-018-1282-8.

Stathopoulou, Georgia, Mark B. Powers, Angela C. Berry, Jasper A. J. Smits, and Michael W. Otto. "Exercise Interventions for Mental Health: A Quantitative and Qualitative Review." *Clinical Psychology: Science and Practice* 13, no. 2 (2006): 179–93.

Stepler, Renee. "Led by Baby Boomers, Divorce Rates Climb for America's 50+ Population." Pew Research Center. Published March 9, 2017. https://www.pew research.org/fact-tank/2017/03/09/led-by-baby-boomers-divorce-rates-climb-for -americas-50-population/.

Takasaki, Kara. "Friends and Family in Relationship Communities: The Importance of Friendship during the Transition to Adulthood." *Michigan Family Review* 1 (2017): 76–96.

Tornello, S. L., B. N. Sonnenberg, and C. J. Patterson. "Division of Labor among Gay Fathers: Associations with Parent, Couple, and Child Adjustment." *Psychology of Sexual Orientation and Gender Diversity* 2, no. 4 (2015): 365–75. https:// doi.org/10.1037/sgd0000109.

Vaillant, George E., Charles C. McArthur, and Arlie Bock. "Grant Study of Adult Development, 1938–2000." *Harvard Dataverse* V4 (2010). https://doi .org/10.7910/DVN/48WRX9.

Voss, Kirsten, Dorothy Markiewicz, and Anna Beth Doyle. "Friendship, Marriage and Self-Esteem." *Journal of Social and Personal Relationships* 16, no. 1 (February 1999): 103–22. https://doi.org/10.1177/0265407599161006.

Wolfinger, Nicholas. "Does Sexual History Affect Marital Happiness?" Institute for Family Studies. 2018. https://ifstudies.org/blog/does-sexual-history-affect -marital-happiness.

INDEX

ABOUT THE AUTHORS

Jessica Griffin, PsyD, is a licensed clinical and forensic psychologist and professor of psychiatry and pediatrics at the University of Massachusetts Chan Medical School, where she has been a faculty member since 2006. Dr. Griffin is a nationally recognized expert in trauma-focused cognitive behavioral therapy (TF-CBT), trauma, and relationships, having trained and provided consultation for thousands of clinicians across the United States. She is the executive director of Lifeline for Kids and the Resilience Through Relationships Center. Under her direction, these programs have trained more than one hundred thousand professionals in trauma-informed care and promoting resilient relationships. She has numerous peer-reviewed publications and is a coauthor on a newly released book by the American Academy of Pediatrics, *Childhood Trauma and Resilience: A Practical Guide*, the first textbook on childhood trauma and resilience for physicians. Dr. Griffin has been featured on NPR, BBC, U.S. News and World Report, Fox News, the *Insider*, Sirius XM Doctor Radio, *People*, *Readers' Digest*, iHeartRadio, the *New York Post*, Medscape, the *Daily Mail*, and hundreds of other news and media outlets. She has served as an expert and consultant on several television docuseries about relationships, marriage, and divorce on A&E's Lifetime television network, including *Seven Year Switch*, *Married at First Sight*, *Honeymoon Island*, and *Happily Ever After*. She has a private consulting and coaching business and is the CEO and co-creator of Love Builder, a relationship company that provides educational online courses to couples, singles, and parents. Dr. Griffin resides in Massachusetts with the loves of her life: her husband, Jon; three children, Carter, Delaney, and Jack; and their two dogs.

Pepper Schwartz, PhD, is a highly acclaimed sociologist who has authored or coauthored more than twenty-five books on intimate relationships, including two *New York Times* best-selling books, *The Normal Bar: The Surprising Secrets of Happy Couples* and, much earlier, *Ten Talks Parents Must Have with Kids about Sex and Character*. Her most recent book, *Snap Strategies: 40 Fast Fixes for Common Relationship Pitfalls*, was picked as one of AARP's honored books. Dr. Schwartz is past president of the Society for the Scientific Study of Sexualities. She has a named fellowship for her work at the University of Washington and an endowed Pepper Schwartz Professorship on Sexuality and Aging at the University of Minnesota. She has appeared in hundreds of news and media outlets and was the original relationship expert on the hit television show *Married at First Sight*. She resides in Washington State and is married to Frederick Kaseburg, the mother of Cooper and Ryder, and the grandmother of Ellie, Noa, Bodie, and Levi.